中国思想文化术语多语种对外翻译
标准化建设项目成果
CHINESE THINKING AND CULTURE
MULTILINGUAL TERMINOLOGY DATABASE

中华源·河南故事
CHINESE CIVILIZATION
Stories from Henan

河洛文化

HELUO CULTURE

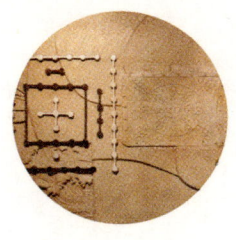

河南省人民政府外事办公室　编

河南大学出版社
HENAN UNIVERSITY PRESS
·郑州·

图书在版编目（CIP）数据

中华源·河南故事．河洛文化：汉、英 / 河南省人民政府外事办公室编．— 郑州：河南大学出版社，2021.4

ISBN 978-7-5649-4667-8

Ⅰ．①中… Ⅱ．①河… Ⅲ．①地方文化－河南－通俗读物－汉、英②文化史－河南－汉、英 Ⅳ．① G127.61-49 ② K296.1

中国版本图书馆 CIP 数据核字（2021）第 076650 号

责任编辑	孙增科
责任校对	屈琳玉
封面设计	翟淼淼
出版发行	河南大学出版社
	地址：郑州市郑东新区商务外环中华大厦2401号　邮编：450046
	电话：0371-86059701（营销部）
	0371-86059750（高等教育与职业教育分公司）
	网址：hupress.henu.edu.cn
排　版	河南大学出版社设计排版部
印　刷	河南博雅彩印有限公司
版　次	2021年4月第1版　　印　次　2021年4月第1次印刷
开　本	710 mm×1010 mm　1/16　印　张　12.5
字　数	200千　　　　　　　　　定　价　62.00元

版权所有，侵权必究

本书如有印装质量问题，请与河南大学出版社营销部联系调换。

"中华源·河南故事"系列丛书编委会

顾　　问	黄友义　杨　平　范大祺
名誉主任	穆为民　何金平　刘炯天
主　　任	付　静
副 主 任	陈　岩　陈志伟　刁玉华　方启雄　介晓磊
	孔留安　李冰冰　李向前　李　镇　梁留科
	刘金锋　牛卫国　屈鹏飞　史永庆　田　凯
	万正峰　王建修　王清义　王自文　许二平
	杨建伟　杨玮斌　张改平　张俊峰　张明超
	张松文　赵卫东

主　　编	付　静
副 主 编	李冰冰
编　　委	陈玮　丁锐　高阳　徐恒振　郑延保

中华源·河南故事·河洛文化

主　　编	陈　岩
副 主 编	刘保亮　段枈卉（英文）
英文译者	韩子满　胡富茂　辛姝泓
英文审校	〔加拿大〕Kizito Tekwa

The Editorial Committee
Chinese Civilization
Stories from Henan

Consultants	Huang Youyi Yang Ping Fan Daqi
Honorary Directors	Mu Weimin He Jinping Liu Jiongtian
Director	Fu Jing
Deputy Directors	Chen Yan Chen Zhiwei Diao Yuhua Fang Qixiong
	Jie Xiaolei Kong Liu'an Li Bingbing Li Xiangqian
	Li Zhen Liang Liuke Liu Jinfeng Niu Weiguo
	Qu Pengfei Shi Yongqing Tian Kai Wan Zhengfeng
	Wang Jianxiu Wang Qingyi Wang Ziwen Xu Erping
	Yang Jianwei Yang Weibin Zhang Gaiping
	Zhang Junfeng Zhang Mingchao Zhang Songwen
	Zhao Weidong
Chief Editor	Fu Jing
Deputy Chief Editor	Li Bingbing
Editors	Chen Wei Ding Rui Gao Yang Xu Hengzhen
	Zheng Yanbao

Chinese Civilization
Stories from Henan
Heluo Culture

Editor-in-Chief	Chen Yan
Associate Editors-in-Chief	Liu Baoliang Duan Aohui(English Text)
Translators	Han Ziman Hu Fumao Xin Shuhong
Translation Proofreaders	Kizito Tekwa (Canada)

总　序

中国是世界四大文明古国之一，也是世界上唯一的古代文明传统未曾中断的国家。河南省地处中国中东部，是中华文明和中华民族的重要发祥地，在中国五千年的文明史上，河南作为国家政治、经济、文化的中心就长达三千多年。从某种意义上讲，一部河南史就是半部中国史。这里是中华人文始祖黄帝的故乡，是古丝绸之路的东方起点，是少林功夫和陈氏太极的发源地，这里创建了中国历史上最早的都城，镌刻了中国最古老的文字，诞生了中国最初的商业文明。

伴随着新时代的荣光，河南经济社会发展迅速，人民生活水平显著提升，这是河南人民自力更生、艰苦奋斗的历史结果，也是对外开放带来的益处。河南经济社会的发展、人民生活方式的改变都植根于深层次的文化积淀。为了让世界更多地了解河南，让河南更好地走向世界，2018年以来，河南省人民政府外事办公室认真研析了这片古老土地上的历史文化资源和时代风貌，组织各领域权威专家学者，编译了"中华源·河南故事"中外文系列丛书，选取黄河文化、河洛文化、老子、庄子、黄帝、少林功夫、太极拳、中医、汉字、丝绸之路、古都、农业、大运河、文物、陶瓷、青铜器、手工艺、书法、杂技、豫菜、豫剧、脱贫攻坚、空中丝绸之路、航空城、南水北调、中国粮谷、红旗渠、焦裕禄等多个主题，力图以故事的方式向世界展现一个立体、全面、真实的河南。

当今世界，人类文明无论是在物质还是在精神方面都取得了巨大进步，特别是物质的极大丰富，这在古代世界是完全不能想象的。同时，当代人类也面临着许多突出的难题，比如，贫富差距持续扩大，物欲追求奢华无度，个人主义恶性膨胀，社会诚信不断消减，伦理道德每况愈下，人与自然关系日趋紧张，等等。要解决这些难题，不仅需要运用人类今天的智慧和力量，而且需要运用人类历史上积累和储存的智慧和力量。河南历史文化底蕴深厚、包容性强，在今天仍极具现实意义。中原文化蕴含的思想智慧有助于修身养性，推动人类社会进步发展，焦裕禄精神、红旗渠精神所体现的为民爱民、艰苦奋斗的价值取向是构建人类命运共同体的力量源泉。我们期待与读者们一起从河南故事中汲取更多的智慧和力量，共同创造更加美好的未来。

Series Foreword

China is one of the four ancient civilizations in the world, and is also the only country in the world where the ancient civilization has not been interrupted. Located in east-central China, Henan Province is an important cradle for the Chinese nation and Chinese civilization. In the course of the five thousand years of Chinese history, for more than three thousand years it served as the political, economic and cultural center of the country and therefore, as generally accepted, represents half of the history of China. Henan is the native place of Yellow Emperor, the cradle of Chinese culture, the starting point of the ancient Silk Road in the east, and the birthplace of Shaolin Kungfu and Chen-style Taijiquan—typical examples of the world-renowned Chinese martial arts. It was here that the earliest capital city in China was founded, the oldest Chinese characters engraved, and the earliest commerce took shape.

In the new era, Henan has witnessed rapid growth in its economy and remarkable improvement of people's living conditions owing to the national reform and opening-up policy and unremitting endeavors of the people. Modern economic achievements and social development as well as the changes of way of life could be traced back to its traditional values and cultural heritages. To enable people from other countries to understand Henan, and let the Province integrate more efficiently into the world development, the Foreign Affairs Office of the People's Government of Henan Province has organized teams of authoritative experts and scholars in relevant fields to compile this *Chinese Civilization: Stories from Henan* in Chinese and foreign languages since 2018 by crystallizing the excellence of traditions and outstanding features of modern development. The book series include *The Yellow River Culture*, *Heluo Culture*, *Laozi*, *Zhuangzi*, *The Yellow Emperor*, *Shaolin Kungfu*, *Taijiquan*, *Traditional Chinese Medicine*,

Chinese Characters, *The Silk Road*, *Ancient Chinese Capitals*, *Feeding the People—Agriculture*, *The Grand Canal*, *Cultural Heritage*, *Ceramic*, *Bronze*, *Handicraft Art*, *Calligraphy*, *Acrobatics*, *Henan Cuisine*, *Henan Opera*, *Poverty Alleviation*, *Silk Road in the Air*, *Zhengzhou—An Aviation City*, *South-to-North Water Diversion*, *China Grain Valley*, *Man-Made River—Hongqiqu Canal*, *A Model Official—Jiao Yulu*, etc., presenting a panoramic picture of the Province.

In today's world, human civilization has made great progress in both material accumulation and ethical advancement, and the great abundance of materials today, especially, is beyond the imagination of the ancient people. At the same time, however, modern people are also confronted with a lot of problems, such as the widening gap between the rich and the poor, the indulgence in pursuit of luxury and extravagance, the undesirable extension of individualism, the decline of social integrity, and the increasingly tense relationship between man and nature. To solve the problems, we need to draw on the wisdom and powers developed today as well as those accumulated in the past. Henan is endowed with rich historical and cultural heritages characterized by its inclusiveness, and such heritages remain significant today. The intelligence and wisdom in Henan culture are conducive to self-cultivation and to the promotion of social development. The spirit of serving the people and relentless struggle, as embodied in Jiao Yulu and Man-Made River—Hongqiqu Canal provides source of strength for building a community with a shared future for mankind. It is our hope that wisdom and strength from Henan stories could lead us to a shared brilliant future.

引 言

在古老的东方大地，黄河一路裂山穿塬，九曲奔流入海，以百折不挠的精神品格哺育着中华民族，孕育了中华文明。黄河是中华民族的母亲河，黄河流域所形成的河湟文化、关中文化、河洛文化、齐鲁文化，共同铸造了中华民族的根和魂。

河洛文化是黄河文化的重要组成部分。"河洛"的"河"指"黄河"，"洛"指"洛河"。从地理范围看，黄河与洛河交汇的河洛地区是以洛阳为中心，东至郑州、开封一带，西界华阴、潼关一线，南至汝颍，北跨黄河而达晋南、济源。但"河洛"不单是一个地域概念，更是一个具有丰富内涵的人文概念。从文化意义看，河洛文化圈的地域影响则涵盖了目前河南省全部地区。需要说明的是，基于河洛文化之中洛阳所占据的中心地位及重要作用，本书论述对象主要聚焦于洛阳，同时参考古代以洛阳为治所的"三川郡""河南尹""河南郡""河南府"等行政区划，把历史上曾受其管辖的巩义、登封、渑池等也纳入视野。

河洛文化的地位独特，是中华文化的源头与核心。河洛地区率先进入文明时代并出现"国家"，成为中华文明的重要发源地。它以"河图""洛书"为标志，体现了中华传统文化的根源性；以夏商周三代文化为主干，体现了中华传统文化的传承性；以洛阳十三朝古都所凝聚的文化精华为核心，体现了中华传统文化的厚重性；以"河洛郎"南迁为途径，体现了中华传统文化的辐射性。儒学起源于洛阳，道学创始于洛阳，佛学首传于洛阳，玄学兴盛于洛阳，理学光大于洛阳。由此，河洛文化不仅是中原的地域文化，而且凝结着中华传统文化的精髓。

黄河滔滔，气势如虹，洛水茫茫，流光溢彩。在黄河流域生态保护和高质量发展上升为国家重大战略的背景下，河洛文化的传承创新在一定意义上"是事关中华民族根和魂的大事"。解读和叙述河洛文化的形成发展与构成要素，不仅能讲好"河南故事""黄河故事"，而且能延续中华历史文脉，坚定文化自信，为实现民族伟大复兴凝聚精神力量。

Introduction

Known as the "mother river" of the Chinese nation, the winding Yellow River in the ancient eastern land runs all the way through plateaus, ravines, and plains before emptying into the Bohai Sea. This indomitable river gave birth to Chinese civilization and continues to nurture the Chinese nation. Hehuang culture (the culture of the people in Hehuang area, Qinghai Province), Guanzhong culture (the culture of the people in central Shaanxi Province), Heluo culture (the culture of the people of Luoyang), and Qilu culture (the culture of the people in Shandong Province) that all originate from the Yellow River Basin jointly constitute the root and soul of the Chinese nation.

Heluo culture is an important component of the Yellow River culture. He, which literally means "river", refers to the Yellow River and luo refers to the "Luohe River." Geographically, the Heluo region that is located at the confluence of the Yellow River and the Luohe River has Luoyang as its center. The region extends to Zhengzhou and Kaifeng in the east, Huayin and Tongguan in the west, the Ru River and the Ying River in the south, southern Shanxi and Jiyuan in the north, on the other side of the Yellow River. However, heluo is not only a regional concept, it is also a humanistic concept with rich meanings. In terms of cultural significance, the regional influence of Heluo culture covers all areas of present-day Henan Province. It should be noted that based on the fact that Luoyang plays the central part in Heluo culture, this book covers not only modern-day Luoyang but also Gongyi, Dengfeng, and Mianchi, which, historically, were once under the jurisdiction of Sanchuan commandery, Henan commandery, and Henan Prefecture that all had Luoyang as their administrative headquarters.

As the cradle and core of Chinese culture, Heluo culture is quite unique in China. The Heluo region led the nation into the era of civilization when the "country" came into being here thereby becoming an important birthplace of

Chinese civilization. It is marked by Hetu and Luoshu(pattern of the Yellow River and Writing of the Luohe River, respectively) that both embody the root of Chinese traditional culture. This culture is chiefly based on the culture of Xia (about 2070 BC–1600 BC), Shang (about1600 BC–1046 BC), and Zhou dynasties (about 1046 BC–256 BC) and it preserves the early achievements of traditional Chinese culture. At its core is the culture of Luoyang City, the capital of thirteen ancient dynasties and a place that profoundly embodies Chinese culture. It is also the starting point of the southward migration of "Heluo Fellows" (Hakka people and their descendants who migrated south from the Heluo region) that clearly marks the dissemination of Chinese traditional culture. Confucianism originated here, Daoism had its beginnings here, Buddhism found its first Chinese destination here, the Weijin metaphysical philosophy flourished here, and Neo-Confucianism thrived here. Thus, Heluo culture is not only the regional culture of the Central Plains but the quintessential traditional Chinese culture.

The Yellow River surges onward like ten thousand galloping horses while Luohe river sprawls forward like brilliant shining stars. As the ecological protection and high-quality development of the Yellow River Basin have become a major national strategy, the inheritance and development of Heluo culture are, in a sense"related to the root and soul of the Chinese nation."The interpretation and description of the development and characteristics of Heluo culture resoundingly tell the Henan story and Yellow River story, as well as carrying on the Chinese historical culture, strengthening cultural self-confidence, and pooling together spiritual strength for the realization of the great rejuvenation of the Chinese nation.

目　录　　　　　　　　　　　　　　　　Contents

第一章　根在河洛　　　　　　　　　　　　001
　　一、河洛古国　　　　　　　　　　　　002
　　二、河图洛书　　　　　　　　　　　　010
　　三、"天下之中"　　　　　　　　　　016
　　四、文明根脉　　　　　　　　　　　　022

Chapter 1　Root in the Heluo Region　　　001
　　Ⅰ. The Ancient Heluo Kingdom　　　　003
　　Ⅱ. Hetu Luoshu　　　　　　　　　　　011
　　Ⅲ. Centre of Heaven and Earth　　　　017
　　Ⅳ. Root of Civilization　　　　　　　023

第二章　古都文化　　　　　　　　　　　　027
　　一、五都荟洛　　　　　　　　　　　　028
　　二、帝都气象　　　　　　　　　　　　038
　　三、帝陵森然　　　　　　　　　　　　048

Chapter 2　Ancient Capital Culture　　　　027
　　Ⅰ. Five Capital Sites in Luoyang　　　029
　　Ⅱ. The Great Royal Capital　　　　　039
　　Ⅲ. Majestic Tombs　　　　　　　　　　049

第三章　思想文化　　　　　　　　　　　　057
　　一、河洛儒学　　　　　　　　　　　　058
　　二、河洛道教　　　　　　　　　　　　064
　　三、河洛佛教　　　　　　　　　　　　070

四、河洛玄学　　080
　　五、河洛理学　　086

Chapter 3　Ideology and Culture　　057
　　Ⅰ. Confucianism in the Heluo Region　　059
　　Ⅱ. Taoism in the Heluo Region　　065
　　Ⅲ. Buddhism in the Heluo Region　　071
　　Ⅳ. Metaphysics in the HeluoRegion　　081
　　Ⅴ. Neo-Confucianism in the Heluo Region　　087

第四章　经济科教　　093
　　一、河洛经济　　094
　　二、河洛科技　　106
　　三、河洛教育　　112

Chapter 4　Economy, Science, Technology, and Education　　093
　　Ⅰ. Economy in the Heluo Region　　095
　　Ⅱ. Science and Technology in the Heluo Region　　107
　　Ⅲ. Education in the Heluo Region　　113

第五章　文学艺术　　119
　　一、河洛文学　　120
　　二、河洛艺术　　130

Chapter 5　Literature and Art　　119
　　Ⅰ. Literature in the Heluo Region　　121
　　Ⅱ. Art in the Heluo Region　　131

第六章　播迁交流　　137
　　一、河洛郎南迁　　138
　　二、向东亚播迁　　146
　　三、沿丝绸之路西传　　156

Chapter 6　The Spread and Exchange of Heluo Culture　　　137
　　　　　Ⅰ. The Migration of Heluo People to the South　　　139
　　　　　Ⅱ. The Spread of Heluo Culture to East Asia　　　147
　　　　　Ⅲ. The Spread of Heluo Culture to the Western Regions Along the
　　　　　　Silk Road　　　157

附录1：河洛文化大事记　　　168
Appendix1: Heluo Cultural Events　　　169

附录2：中国历史年代简表　　　182
Appendix2: A Brief Chronology of Chinese History　　　182

第一章

根在河洛

Chapter 1

Root in the Heluo Region

河洛文化具有"根文化"的重要特征。以炎黄二帝为代表的中华人文始祖,作为中华文明的发轫者,他们大都出自或主要活动于河洛地区,华夏部族最先脱离了野蛮蒙昧时代,迈进了文明的门槛。以双槐树遗址为中心"河洛古国"的考古发现,"河图洛书"的文献记载,"天下之中"的人文地理观念,无不肇始了"最早的中国"。"根在河洛",表明河洛地区不仅最早闪现出中华文明的第一线曙光,而且也是华夏民族最初的发源形成之地。

一、河洛古国

中华文明作为世界四大文明之一,是唯一延续至今未曾中断的,它如何起源、发展备受关注。中华文明五千年究竟只是个传说,还是真实的历史?无论是国家"夏商周断代工程",还是随后的"中华文明探源工程",都试图回答这一问题。2020年5月7日,郑州市文物考古研究院公布了双槐树遗址重大考古成果。这一有关黄帝时期"河洛古国"的考古成果,完美地诠释了中华五千年的文明信史。

双槐树遗址位于黄河南岸高台地上、伊洛河汇流入黄河处的河南巩义河洛镇,处于河洛文化中心区。遗址面积达117万平方米,发现有仰韶文化中晚阶段的大型中心居址、大型连片块状夯土遗迹、三处经过严格规划的大型公共墓地、三处夯土祭祀台遗迹等,并出土了一大批仰韶文化时期丰富的文化遗物。

北斗九星天文遗迹。在双槐树遗址的中心居址区内,发现有4排大型房址,房址之间有巷道相通,其中最大的一个房子的门廊处,发现了用九个陶罐摆放成北斗星的形状。北斗七星,有时也叫作北斗九星。北斗九星天文遗迹的发现,表明5000多年前的"北斗"崇拜是当时仰韶先民的最高信仰之一,也说明当时人们已经具有相对成熟的"天象授时观"。同时,由于中心居址区为"河洛古国"的贵族活动区域,主人用

The most important characteristic of the Heluo culture is its consideration as the root and ancestor culture. Represented by the two emperors, Yan and Huang, who were the pioneers of Chinese civilization, most of the Chinese ancestors came from or mainly lived in the Heluo region. Huaxia became the civilized tribe in the central part of China. The discovery, by archeologists, of the ancient Heluo Kingdom with the Shuanghuaishu site at its center, the recordings of Hetu and Luoshu in historical documents, and the humanistic geographic concept of the center of Heaven and Earth, all point to the fact that Luoyang was home to "the earliest China." The notion of root in Heluo region indicates that the Heluo region is a testimony not only to the first ray of Chinese civilization, but also the birth of the Huaxia nation.

I. The Ancient Heluo Kingdom

As one of the four major civilizations in the world, the Chinese civilization is the only civilization that has persisted till today without interruption, and its origin and development have attracted considerable attention. Is the 5000-year-old Chinese civilization just a legend or a truth? Both the Xia-Shang-Zhou Chronology Project and the subsequent Origins of Chinese Civilization Project have attempted to answer this question. On May 7, 2020, Zhengzhou Institute of Cultural Heritage and Archaeology announced its major archaeological findings in the Shuanghuaishu site. These archaeological findings of the ancient Heluo Kingdom during the Yellow Emperor period (2717 BC–2599 BC) perfectly testified to more than 5,000 years of Chinese history.

Lying on the tableland of the south bank of the Yellow River in the township of Heluo, Gongyi City, Henan Province, the Shuanghuaishu site is located at the center of Heluo region at the confluence of the Yellow River and the Luohe River. Tremendous historic and cultural relics of the Yangshao period (about 7000 to 5000 years ago) were unearthed in the ruins which covered a large area of 1.17 million square meters. In the area were unearthed the ruins of the central residential area of the mid-late stage of Yangshao culture (about 7000 to 5000 years ago). Additionally, rammed-earth foundations of large courtyards, three scientifically planned public cemeteries, three sacrificial remains, and other

北斗九星来神话自己，表达自己是呼应天上中心的地下王者。

在北斗九星遗迹上端，北极附近，还有一头首向南并朝着门道的完整麋鹿骨架。古代天子有冬至祭天的传统，而麋鹿在古人眼里是一种神奇的动物。大部分鹿类在夏天脱角，只有麋鹿在冬至脱角，所以统治者把麋鹿脱角视为吉祥的象征，并把麋鹿与一年最重要的节气冬至关联。九个陶罐和麋鹿都埋在地下，当房子建成后，居住的主人日常活动时，就仿佛骑在麋鹿身上，这应该是一位有地位并且谙习巫术和天文的古国首领，以此神化自己，向诸部落氏族宣誓权力掌控。

中国最早的骨质蚕雕。遗址出土的骨质蚕雕这件艺术品长6.4厘米，宽不足1厘米，厚0.1厘米，用野猪獠牙雕刻而成，是一条正在吐丝的家蚕形象。它的做工十分精致，腹足、胸足、头部组合明晰，和现代的家蚕极为相似，同时背部凸起，头昂尾翘，与蚕吐丝或即将吐丝时的造型高度契合。这是迄今发现的仰韶时期与养蚕及丝绸起源相关联的、比较直观的实物资料。它与青台遗址等周边同时期遗址出土的迄今最早丝绸实物一起，实证了5300年前后黄河中游地区的先民们已经养蚕缫丝。北京大学教授、夏商周断代工程首席科学家李伯谦认为，中华文明的一个典型特征即是农桑文明、丝帛文明。中国新石器时代各地代表性文化的农业都较为发达，但在距今5300年前后，除了双槐树为首的聚落，全国其他地方却没有与桑蚕纺织业有关的确切发现。从这一角度讲，以双槐树遗址为首的黄河流域中心聚落群，是目前发现的中国农桑文明发展史上时代最早的代表。

图1-1　骨质蚕雕

Figure 1-1　A Boar Tusk Carving of a Silkworm

facilities were also discovered.

Astronomical relics of the Big Dipper Nine Stars. In the central residential area of the Shuanghuaishu site, four rows of big houses separated by roadways were found. At the porch of the biggest of those houses, nine pottery pots were arranged in the pattern of the nine stars of the Big Dipper. The Big Dipper is also called the Big Dipper Nine Stars. The relics indicate that Yangshao ancestors worshipped the Big Dipper and that Heluo ancestors had relatively mature astronomical knowledge by being able to carry out agricultural activities based on their observation of celestial phenomena. Meanwhile, given that the central residential area was the administrative region of the royal court in the ancient Heluo kingdom, the palace monarch considered the Big Dipper Nine Stars as a symbol of himself and used them to showcase his supremacy over all other human beings.

At the top of the relics of the Big Dipper Nine Stars, near the north pole, there is a complete skeleton of an elk, with its head to south, pointing to the gate. In ancient times, the emperor would follow the tradition of offering sacrifices to heaven on the winter solstice, and the elk was a magical animal in the eyes of the ancients. Most of the deer shed their horns in summer, and only the elk shed their horns on the winter solstice. Therefore, the rulers regarded the elk shedding as a symbol of auspiciousness, and associated the elk with the winter solstice, the most important solar term of the year. The nine earthenware pots and the elk were all buried under the ground. When the house was built, the owner of the house seemed to ride on back of the elk in his daily activities. This should be a leader of an ancient country who was in high position and was familiar with witchcraft and astronomy, so as to deify himself and swear to all the tribal clans for power.

China's earliest bone carving depicting a spinning silkworm. Among the unearthed relics, there is a boar tusk carving of a silkworm measuring 6.4 cm long, nearly 1 cm wide, and 0.1 cm thick. With clear pleopods, pereiopods, and a head and with its back hunching and a head and tail up, the delicate artwork depicts a spinning silkworm that appears strikingly identical to modern silkworms. The relic is also valuable material related to the origin of silk and silkworm breeding in the Yangshao period (about 7000 to 5000 years ago) that has, so far, been discovered. Furthermore, silk fabrics unearthed at the surrounding Qingtai site are solid

图1-2 双槐树遗址示意

Figure 1-2　The Shuanghuaishu Site

evidence of the fact that ancient Chinese in the middle reaches of the Yellow River basin began silkworm breeding and silk reeling around 5,300 years ago. Li Boqian, professor at Peking University and chief scientist of the Xia-Shang-Zhou Chronology Project, believes that the mulberry-growing and silkworm-raising culture was an important component of Chinese civilization. In the Neolithic Age of China (about 5,000 to 2,000 years ago), agriculture in all representative local cultures of China was relatively developed. However, outside Shuanghuaishu and its surrounding settlements, there have been no proven discoveries related to the silk textile industry over the past 5,300 years. That means, Shuanghuaishu and its surrounding settlements are the earliest representatives in the history of Chinese mulberry cultivation and silkworm-rearing culture.

Additionally, three public cemeteries with more than 1,700 rows of Yangshao period (about 7000 to 5000 years ago) tombs were found at the site. The tombs lie in the east-west direction and those buried in them lie on their backs, their heads facing west and their limbs stiffened up. The main body of one of the burial areas was surrounded by the outer and middle ring trenches of the site and a moat, an apparent embryonic form of the emperor mausoleum system in China.

The artifacts unearthed at the Shuanghuaishu site contain many other cultural elements. For instance, Zhefu Ding (red pottery tripod with inscribed circles of lines on upper contracted belly and neck) and Bei Hu (pottery pot with a small round mouth, a long neck, a sloping shoulder, an eagle-shaped button on the bulging belly tapering downwards and two opposite ears in the shape of a ring) carry the features of Dawenkou culture. A great deal of double-belly wares unearthed, such as double-belly *pen* (pottery basin with a square mouth, circles of lines on the upper contracted part in the middle of the belly and flat bottom), double-belly *dou* (ancient pottery food vessel with a contracted design in the middle of the belly and a high round foot in openwork technique), double-belly *wan* (pottery bowl with a wide mouth, contracted design in the middle of the belly and a flat bottom), and egg-shell painted pottery cup with a wide mouth, sloping belly, and small base have elements of Qujialing culture. The cultural element of hook-shaped implement made of deer antler at Shuangdun site in Shuangdun Village, Anhui Province, and Zhefu Bei (pottery cup with a wide mouth and a contracted belly) at Xuejiagang site were also found in the relics

遗址内发现3处墓葬区，共有1700多座仰韶文化时期的墓葬，均呈排状分布。墓葬为东西向，墓主人仰身直肢，头向西。其中一个墓葬区早期主体被遗址外壕和中壕及一条围沟围成一个独立的区域，应是中国早期帝王陵寝兆域制度的雏形。

双槐树遗址的出土器物，包含许多外来文化因子。如折腹鼎、背壶具备大汶口文化特征；陶器组合中出现的大量双腹器，如双腹盆、双腹豆、双腹碗，以及薄胎斜腹彩陶杯，属于屈家岭文化因素；还可以看到双墩文化靴形器、薛家岗文化折腹杯、大溪文化杯等文化元素。这些器物充分证明，河洛地区在距今5000年前后就是联通四方的交通要道。

中华文明可分为古国时代、王国时代和帝国时代。以往国内大部分学者虽然肯定河洛地区在中华文明起源中的地位和作用，但认为河洛的中心地位是从夏代才开始的，并不赞同更早的时候也具有中心地位。以"河洛古国"命名的双槐树遗址的考古发现，其宏大的建筑规模，严谨有序的布局，所表现的社会发展模式和承载的思想观念，无不呈现出古国时代的王都气象，它实证了在5300年前后这一中华文明起源的黄金阶段，河洛地区是当时最具代表性和影响力的文明中心。在这一阶段，虽然文化上的中国已经形成雏形，而河洛古国则堪称"早期中华文明的胚胎"。其天地之中的宇宙观、合天命而治的礼仪性思维、具有引领性的文明发展模式，被后世所承袭和发扬，五千多年中华文明正是赖此主根脉延续不断、瓜瓞绵绵。

discovered at the Shuanghuaishu site. These artifacts fully prove that about 5000 years ago, Heluo region was a transportation hub that connected all parts of the country.

  Chinese civilization can be divided into ancient civilization, kingdom reign and the imperial era. Although most experts in China affirmed the position and role of Heluo region in the origin of Chinese civilization in the past, they thought that the essential role of Heluo region was established in the Xia Dynasty(about 2070 BC — 1600 BC) and did not agree with the statement that it was in the central position much earlier than previously known. The archaeological finding of the Shuanghuaishu site was named ancient Heluo Kingdom based on its grand scale, typical and organized layout, social development model, and ideology which show the flourishment and magnificence of the kingdom in ancient times. The significant relics prove the representativeness and influence of the Heluo region in the golden stage of the origin of Chinese civilization around 5,300 years ago. At this stage, although the rudiment of China came into being from the cultural perspective, the ancient "Heluo Kingdom" was recognized as the embryo of early Chinese civilization by experts and scholars. The universal concept of the center of Heaven and Earth, the ritual thinking of governance according to the principles of nature, and the leading development model of civilization have been inherited and carried forward by following generations. It is precisely on this basis that the Chinese civilization has continued for more than 5,000 years.

二、河图洛书

"河图"与"洛书"产生于河洛地区。《易·系辞上》曰:"河出图,洛出书,圣人则之。""河出图",传说在上古伏羲氏时,在今洛阳东北孟津县境内的黄河中浮出龙马,背负"河图",献给伏羲。今天在孟津县东北10公里黄河南岸雷河村,有一条流入黄河的图河,沿岸有卦沟、负图、上河图等与传说相关的诸多村名,当地村民认为这里就是当年伏羲氏降服龙马、受河图而画八卦的地方。雷河村南边有一座龙马负图寺,是"龙马负图"在孟津的一个佐证。"洛出书",据说大禹时代有神龟从洛水出现,背负"洛书",献给大禹。在今洛阳洛宁县洛水岸边的长水村内,立有两通"洛出书处"古碑,村西南的龙头山上现存有始建于北宋时期的禹王庙,附近还有"仓颉造字台"遗址。"圣人则之",圣人是指伏羲、大禹,《汉书·五行传》中刘歆认为:"伏羲氏继天而王,受《河图》,则而画之,八卦是也。禹治洪水,赐《雒(洛)书》,法而陈之,《洪范》是也。"这样河图洛书与儒家的两部经典《周易》《尚书》建立了内在的关联。

河图、洛书是中国古代的两幅神秘图案。河图、洛书在先秦、西汉的典籍中有其文字记载。以后,在汉代刘歆、孔安国、扬雄、班固等人的著作中也屡有提及。但河图、洛书到底是个什么样子,这些文献上都没有明确说明。今天看到的用圆圈和黑点组成的河图洛书图,最早著录于南宋朱熹《周易本义》的卷首,据说是从五代道士陈抟那里流传出来的。

II. Hetu Luoshu

The birthplace of Hetu (Yellow River chart) and Luoshu (Luo River inscription) was in the Heluo region. The first volume of Xici from *The Book of Changes* explains that the sage rulers read and interpreted the Yellow River Chart as well as the Inscription of the River Luo and modeled their reign according to the evidence provided in the two diagrams. It is said that in ancient times, when Fuxi (Chinese mythological emperor) was born, a Longma (dragonhorse) emerged out of the Yellow River in Mengjin County, northeast of Luoyang, carrying Hetu for Fuxi. Today, in Leihe Village that is located 10 km northeast of Mengjin County on the south bank of the Yellow River, Tuhe River flows into the Yellow River. Along Tuhe River, some villages are named after legends including the Eight Trigrams and Hetu. Local villagers believed that this is the place Fu xi subdued the dragon-horse, received the Hetu and drew Bagua (Eight Trigrams). There is a temple named Longmafutu which commemorates the legend according to which the dragon-horse jumped out of the Yellow River, carrying the Hetu in the south of Leihe Village, proving the existence of this legend in Mengjin. As for Luoshu, it is said that the God Turtle appeared from the LuoRiver and carried the Luoshu for Yu the Great. In Changshui Village on the bank of the LuoRiver in Luoning County, Luoyang, there are two ancient monuments of Luoshu. On Longtou Mountain in the southwest of the village, there is a temple of Yu the Great built during the Northern Song Dynasty, and a nearby site where Cangjie invented the Chinese character. The sage rulers in *The Book of Changes*, it should be noted, refer to Fuxi and Yu the Great. Liu Xin in the chapter "WuxingZhuan" (Treatise on the Five Agents) from *The Book of Han* maintained that Fuxi drew Bagua based on Hetu, and Yu the Great put forward nine categories in the Grand Norm to govern the nation according to the evidence provided by Luoshu in his endeavor to control the flood. Therefore, Hetu Luoshu has established an internal connection with the two Confucian classics, *The Book of Changes* and *The Book of History*.

Hetu and Luoshu are two mysterious patterns in ancient China. There are written records about Hetu Luoshu in books and records of the pre-Qin period

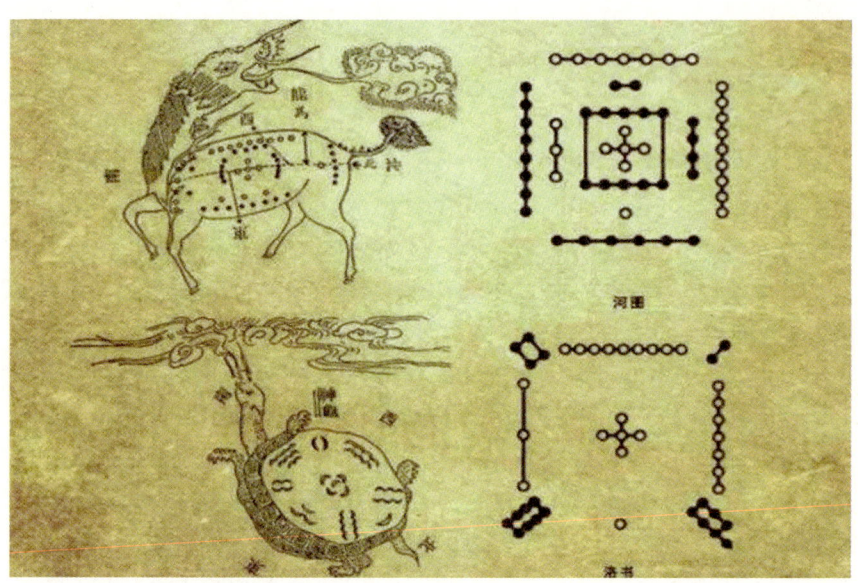

图1-3 河图洛书
Figure 1-3　Hetu Luoshu

河图洛书是中国易文化的本源。《周易》和《礼纬》对其均有记载。河图和洛书结合在一起，奠定了《周易》哲学思想的基础。《史记·周本纪》记载，周文王曾经被商纣王囚禁于河洛地区的羑里（今河南汤阴），在此期间他将伏羲所画的八卦，两两相重，形成六十四卦。他还将六十四卦按一定的哲学思想排列次序，每卦都做了简要说明，称为"卦辞"。东汉经学发达，《易》居"五经"首位，帝都洛阳无疑是易学的第一重镇。从易学文化初创到北宋兴盛的漫长历史时期，可以说它都没有完全离开河洛地区而独立发展。

河图洛书是河洛文化的滥觞。它虽然是一个争论不休的千载难解之谜，无论是在先秦被认为是一种祥瑞之兆，还是在两汉成为"龙马负图""神龟贡书"的神话传说与谶纬之学，抑或到了宋代演化为黑白点数图式，以及今天又有河洛先民图腾信仰的新解，但这众说纷纭的论争并不影响其成为中华文化的元典，并于2014年12月"河图洛书传说"正式入选国家级非物质文化遗产名录。河图洛书开启了"天人合一"的中

(2,100 BC–221 BC) and the Western Han Dynasty(206 BC–24 AD). Later, in the Han Dynasty (206 BC–220 AD), Liu Xin, Kong Anguo, Yang Xiong, Ban Gu and others made multiple references to their works. However, there is no clear explanation in these documents as to what HetuLuoshu looks like. The Hetu and Luoshu diagrams, composed of circles and black spots, were first recorded in the frontispiece of Zhu Xi's *ZhouyiBenyi* (the original meaning of *The Book of Changes*) in the Southern Song Dynasty and is said to have been handed down from Chen Tuan, a Taoist priest in the Five Dynasties.

Hetu Luoshu is the origin of Chinese Yi (Changes) culture. It is recorded in *The Book of Changes* and *Liwei*(a prophecy book published in the Han Dynasty). The combination of Hetu and Luoshu laid the philosophical foundation of *The Book of Changes*. It is recorded in the chapter dedicated to the Zhou Dynasty from the *Records of the Historian* that King Wen of Zhou (1100BC–1050 BC) was once imprisoned by King Zhou of Shang (1075BC–1046 BC) in Youli (present-day Tangyin, Henan Province) in the Heluo region. During that period, he combined the Bagua (8 trigrams) drawn by Fuxi into 64 hexagrams. He also arranged 64 hexagrams in a certain philosophical order and the brief explanation of each hexagram became what was known as the divinatory text. The study of Confucian classics thrived in the Eastern Han Dynasty, and Yiology ranked first among the Five Classics. Luoyang, the imperial city, was undoubtedly the first important city in the study of Yiology. In the Northern Song Dynasty (960–1127), during the long historical period from its beginning to its prosperity, Yiology developed exclusively inside the Heluo region.

Hetu Luoshu is the origin of Heluo culture. Although it has been a long-debated mystery, whether it was regarded as an auspicious omen in the pre-Qin period, or a myth and divination during the Han Dynasty, or a black-and-white point schema in the Song Dynasty (960–1279), and despite the novel interpretation of the totem belief of Heluo ancestors today, such controversy does not affect its success in the Chinese culture. In December 2014, Legend of Hetu Luoshu was officially included in the national intangible cultural heritage list. Hetu Luoshu marked the start of harmony between man and nature in Chinese culture, reflecting the worship of numbers and the concept of time and space in ancient times. It also indicated the recognition, by ancestors, of astronomy,

华文化导向，反映出远古时期的数字崇拜和时空观念，表现了古代先民所具有的天文、地理、人伦、哲学、艺术、原始宗教、日常生活等方方面面的认知，是其在长期的生产实践和社会活动中，外观天地物象，内察社会人事，探讨各自的消长变化，研究彼此之间的关系和影响，而所总结出的天地规律及辩证智慧。河图洛书的文化贡献，至今仍闪耀着神秘的光辉。

geography, human relations, philosophy, art, primitive religion, daily life, and other aspects. In its long-term production practice and social activities, it has summed up the laws of heaven and earth and dialectical wisdom by viewing the images of heaven, earth, and objective things, observing social and human relations, discussing their ups and downs, and studying the relationship and influence among them. The contribution of Hetu Luoshu in Chinese culture still shines with mysterious brilliance.

三、"天下之中"

"天下之中"思想与五帝和夏商时期人类对宇宙秩序的认识有密切的渊源关系。在中国先民看来，作为空间之宇宙是规范而有序的，中央高于四方，乃宇宙秩序的轴心。这样的观念延伸到社会领域时，在部落或酋邦时代，人们就会以自我为中心去构想世界秩序。

黄帝相传居天下之中。《淮南子·天文训》说："中央土也，其帝黄帝，其佐后土，执绳而制四方。"这种以"土"居中央，以黄帝为统领四方之帝的理路，所遵循的即"尚中"原则。夏代据《禹贡》记载，夏禹平水土，更制九州，中州之外有八方。商朝以五方观念将全国政治疆域划分为五方，商王直接统治区居中，号称"中商"。河图洛书是"天下之中"思想的重要源头之一，与其有内在关联的《周易》中，"中"的出现频率高达119次，六十四卦中过半数的"传"之内容，都涉及了"中"。五帝和夏商周三代形成的"尚中"观念，成为"天下之中"思想的基点，对当时和后世产生了深刻影响。

洛阳为"天下之中"，是周公营建洛邑时明确提出的。《史记·周本纪》记载，他在陈述选择洛阳地区兴建成周时说："此天下之中，四方入贡道里均。"《逸周书·作雒》也提到周公"作大邑成周于土中""以为天下之大凑"。土中即大地之中，天下之凑是说这里是八方辐辏之地，是朝会、贡赋、交通和商业的中心。这里周公强调都城建在天下之中，表明"中"对于王权和国家具有特殊意义，既有利于发挥都城的聚集和扩散作用，也易于形成周边对中央王朝的依附和归顺。周公营建洛邑提出并阐发了"天下之中"理论，遂使其成为一种建都选址的重要标准，并使其由一般的地理空间概念上升到政治文化思想的高度。

"天下之中"思想是汉唐之间列朝都洛的一个重要因素。东汉刘秀"复帝祚，迁都雒阳，以服土中"，他不仅看中了洛阳"天下之中"的

III. Centre of Heaven and Earth

The thought of the center of heaven and earth is closely related to the understanding of the order of the universe in the era of the Five Emperors (2852 BC–2205 BC) and Xia and Shang dynasties (2100 BC–1046 BC). From the perspective of Chinese ancestors, the universe, conceived as space, has its law and order, with the center, which is the axis of the universe order, higher than the four sides. With such an understanding of the social practice, people in the era of tribes and chiefdoms tended to consider themselves as the center in their conception of world order.

Legend has it that the Yellow Emperor lived in the center of the world. It is laid out in the chapter dedicated to Tianwenxun (celestial patterns) in *the book of Master Huainan*, that "the Centre is Earth. Its god is the Yellow Emperor. His assistant is Hou Tu. He grasps the marking cord and governs the four quarters" This kind of principle, which takes the earth as the center and the Yellow Emperor as the leader of the four sides, is called the principle of "esteeming the center." According to Yu Gong (Tribute of Yu, a chapter of *the Book of History*), Yu the Great governed the nine provinces, including the middle region and the other eight regions outside the middle region. In the Shang Dynasty, the political territory was divided into five communities and states. The area the king of Shang directly ruled was in the middle and was called Zhongshang (the center of Shang's reign). Hetu Luoshu is one of the important sources of the concept of center of heaven and earth. In *The Book of Changes*, which is intrinsically linked to this thought, the frequency of occurrence of the character *the Book of History* (center or middle) is as high as 119 times, and more than half of the contents of Zhuan in 64 hexagrams are related to *zhong*. The concept of "esteeming the center" formed in the period of the Five Emperors and the Xia, Shang, and Zhou dynasties transformed to the primary idea of center of heaven and earth and had a profound impact on later generations.

The concept that Luoyang was the center of heaven and earth, was clearly put forward by Zhou Gong (Duke of Zhou) when he built Luoyi (an ancient Chinese city located in Luoyang during the Zhou Dynasty). According to the

图1-4 周公营造洛邑 刘龙/摄

Figure 1-4 Statue of the Duke of Zhou, founder of Luoyi, today's Luoyang Photo by Liu Long

chapter dedicated to the Zhou Dynasty from *The Records of the Historian*, in the explanation of the location of Chengzhou City (the site of the ancestral temple) in Luoyang area, it is claimed that "in the center of the world, this location is convenient for vassal states to pay tribute." In the *Yi Zhou Shu* (a compendium of Chinese historical documents about the Western Zhou period from 1046BC–771 BC), it was also mentioned that Zhou Gong chose this as the gathering place, the center of the court, the tribute center, and the center of transportation and commerce. Zhou Gong stressed the geographical importance of the capital city, an indication that "center" was of special significance to the royal power and the country. It was not only a convenient meeting point for the nation, but also a strategic starting point to subdue and conquer the surrounding areas. Zhou Gong put forward and expounded the theory of *center of heaven and earth* when he built Luoyi thereby transforming the concept into an important benchmark in the location of the capital and raising it from the general concept of geographical space to the realm of political and cultural ideology.

The idea of choosing the center of heaven and earth was an important consideration in the choice of Luoyang as capital in the Han and Tang dynasties. Liu Xiu (Emperor Guangwu) established the Eastern Han Dynasty with his capital at Luoyang. He not only valued Luoyang's geographical location as the center, but also viewed Luoyang's political and cultural advantages as center. He inherited the administrative system of the Zhou Dynasty, valued civility and literature as well as frugality and benevolent government. The status and significance of Luoyang's geographical importance have been recognized by both the rulers of Han nationality and the rulers of the ethnic minorities. The decision to establish Luoyang as its capital has become an important part of the Chinesization process. The relocation of its capital to Luoyang in the Northern Wei Dynasty constitutes a good example. Emperor Xiaowen moved the capital to the central areas as he thought highly of the civility and culture of the Central Plains in his endeavor to position himself in the historical order and realistic pattern of China and establish the legitimacy of the Northern Wei regime in China. The capital of the Sui Dynasty was Chang'an and after Emperor Yang of Sui acceded to the throne, he decided to build a new capital. His imperial edict said that, " Luoyi, the center of heaven and earth and the convergence of Yin and

地理位置，更看中的是洛阳"天下之中"的政治文化优势，既继承"周制"，修文偃武，崇尚节俭，实行德政。洛阳"天下之中"的地位和意义，不仅得到汉族统治者的认可，也得到少数民族统治者的认同，少数民族统治者建都洛阳的行为，实际上也成为其汉化过程的一个重要内容。北魏迁都于洛就是一个很好的例证。北魏孝文帝以中原为正统，神州为帝宅，以此争取在华夏历史顺序和现实格局中的位置，确立北魏政权在华夏的正统性、合法性地位。隋朝本都长安，隋炀帝即位后，决定营建新都，其诏曰："洛邑自古之都，王畿之内，天地之所合，阴阳之所和。控以三河，固以四塞，水陆通，贡赋等。故汉祖曰：'吾行天下多矣，唯见洛阳'……今可于伊、洛营建东京。"唐代高宗首幸洛阳，就看中了"此都中兹宇宙，通赋贡于四方；交乎风雨，均朝宗于万国"的"天下之中"地位，将洛阳宫改称东都，并定东西都所在官员阶品相等。武后执政，改唐为周，以洛阳为"神都"，其所发布的诏诰表明她对"天下之中"理论的认同。隋唐建都洛阳，在地理形势上是向东扩展、转移，在文化形态上则是力图利用洛阳"天下之中"的文化优势，缩小东西、南北文化的差异，这与当年周公在洛阳制礼作乐、构建统一的周文化体系有着相同旨趣。

"天下之中"是河洛文化的一个重要思想，对于华夏民族有着不可磨灭的影响。它不仅以中间、中心对称为美塑造着中国人的思维模式与审美倾向，而且封建社会更是长期借助人们对"天地之中"的敬畏崇拜证明与巩固"君权神授"的"合法性"。"天下之中"建都理论所表现出的空间意识和文化观念，还顽强地深入中华民族的灵魂之中，发展出一种中和、中庸的哲学与伦理思想。"天下之中"是一种凝固的空间意识、历史意识、民族意识，在一定意义上是中华民族之伟大凝聚力与向心力的表现。

Yang was the capital in ancient times. Commanding three rivers and protected by four surrounding forts, with convenient water and land transportation, Luoyang was a good place to collect tax and tributes. Therefore, Emperor Gaozu of the Han Dynasty said, 'I have traveled all over the world, and Luoyang is the best'…Today, I can build the eastern capital along the Yihe and Luohe River. " When the Emperor Gao Zong of Tang first visited, he was attracted to Luoyang because of its superior geographical location at the center and because it was convenient to collect tribute from all sides. So, Luoyang city was renamed the Eastern Capital, and the officials in Eastern and Western capitals were equal in rank and grade. When Wu Hou (an Empress regnant) came into power, she changed the Tang Dynasty to the Zhou Dynasty, and made Luoyang the capital. The imperial edict issued by Wu Hou approved the central location and importance of Luoyang. As a result, Luoyang, the capital of Sui and Tang dynasties, expanded and shifted geographically eastward. Such a capital site selection was an attempt to take advantage of Luoyang's cultural advantages in the center to narrow the cultural differences between the east and west as well as the north and south. This was consistent with Zhou Gong's construction of a unified cultural system of the Zhou Dynasty in Luoyang.

  The center of heaven and earth is an important philosophy of Heluo culture that has had an indelible influence on the Chinese nation. It has shaped the thinking of Chinese people and their aesthetic tendency with asymmetrical beauty while espousing and consolidating the legitimacy of the divine right of kings through the people's awe and continuous worship, within the feudal society, of the center of heaven and earth. The spatial consciousness and cultural concept outlined in the capital construction theory of "the center" have also deeply penetrated the Chinese nation and developed a philosophy and ethical thought of neutralization and moderation. The center of heaven and earth is a kind of solidified space, a historical and national consciousness, which, in a sense, is the expression of the great cohesion and centripetal force of the Chinese nation.

四、文明根脉

河洛地区早在旧石器时代就是人类重要的活动地带。新石器时代的裴李岗文化、仰韶文化、龙山文化、二里头文化都在河洛地区有典型的遗存。距今七千年到五千年的仰韶文化，是以河洛地区渑池县仰韶村遗址命名的。洛阳王湾遗址、孙旗屯遗址、锉李遗址，特别是以"河洛古国"命名的双槐树遗址，都是仰韶文化时期典型的先民聚落地，证明在距今五六千年前，河洛地域已经是村落棋布、人口密集的地区，河洛先民在这里过着相对稳定的农业定居生活。

炎帝和黄帝是中华民族的人文始祖，炎黄文化是中华文化的母体。炎黄二族是由少典、有蟜两大氏族部落裂变而来的。有蟜氏是以蜜蜂为图腾的部落，他们活动的中心是洛阳附近的平逢山。有蟜氏在洛阳，那么与之通婚的少典氏不应该离此太远，也应在洛阳地区。《竹书纪年》曰："黄帝祭于洛水"，帝尧"祭于洛"，"沉璧于洛"。河洛地带自古是我国炎黄始祖的活动中心。

20世纪以来，考古发现了中国古代文明的本土起源和多中心发展的基本特点。登封王城岗等城址的考古发现，表明大约在距今4300年前，河洛地区汇聚了各地先进的文化因素，开始显现出领先的态势，并最终促成了二里头广域王权国家的形成。从此在相当长的时期内，河洛地区成为中国古代文明的核心和根基。

河洛文化是华夏文明的根脉，还表现于河洛地区是中华宗亲祖居，是中华姓氏重要的起源地。先秦时代，姓、氏有别，秦汉以后，姓、氏合一，通称为姓，一直延续至今。黄帝故里在河洛地区，依据《世本》对黄帝后代的粗略统计：黄帝有子25人，得姓者有12姓。从黄帝时代到先秦时期，黄帝直系子族发展到101个属地（方国、诸侯国），共分衍出501个氏。这些黄帝后裔繁衍的姓氏，是当今中华民族姓氏的重要组

IV. Root of Civilization

Heluo region was an important area of human activities as early as the Paleolithic times. There are typical remains and relics of Neolithic time Peiligang culture, Yangshao culture, Longshan culture, and Erlitou culture in Neolithic time. Yangshao culture, dating back 7,000 to 5,000 years, was named after the ruins of Yangshao Village in Mianchi County, Heluo Prefecture. Luoyang Wangwan site, sunqitun site, and Cuoli Site, and especially the Shuanghuaishu site, which is named after Heluo Kingdom, are all typical ancestral settlements during the Yangshao culture period. This evidence proves that about 5,000 to 6,000 years ago, Heluo region was already a densely populated area comprised of villages where Heluo ancestors lived a relatively stable agricultural-based life.

Yan Emperor and Huang Emperor are the humanistic ancestors of the Chinese nation, and Yan Huang culture gave birth to the Chinese culture. The two tribes under the leadership of Yan Emperor and Huang Emperor are descendants of the Shaodian and Youjiao clans. With bees as its totem, the Youjiao clan resided around Pingfeng Mountain near Luoyang. That means the geographical location of the Shaodian clan, who intermarried with the Youjiao clan, should not be too far away, probably also in the Luoyang area. It was recorded in *Bamboo Annals* that Huang Emperor and Yao Emperor offered sacrifices by Luohe River. Ever since ancient times, the Heluo region has been the activity center of Yanhuang ancestors.

Since the 20th century, the origin of ancient Chinese civilization and the basic characteristics of multi-center development have been discovered in archaeology. Archaeological discoveries at Wangchenggang site in Dengfeng and other cities indicate that Heluo region gathered advanced cultural elements from all over the country and began to show a leading trend about 4,300 years ago. This trend eventually contributed to the formation of Erlitou's wide-area kingship country. Ever since, Heluo region has become the core and basis of ancient Chinese civilization for a long time.

This is also reflected in the fact that Heluo region is the ancestral home of Chinese clansmen and an important origin of Chinese surnames. In the pre-Qin period, the *xing* (family name to show genetic inheritance) and *shi* (name to

成部分。据统计，中国自古至今出现过22000多个姓氏（现在仍使用的至少有3500多个），其中起源于河南省的约占三分之二。

河洛文化是华夏文明的根脉，"最早的中国"是其有力表征。"中国"一词的最初含义，是指洛阳一带。据考证，"中国"一词，最早出现于1965年陕西宝鸡出土的西周初年青铜器"何尊"的铭文里，有"余其宅兹中国，自之辟民"等语。铭文中的"中国"，即指周王朝疆域的成周地区，也即今天的洛阳一带。由此，洛阳一带称为"中土"或"土中"，后来河南省也被称为"中州"或"中原"。中国社科院考古研究所研究员、夏商周考古研究室主任兼二里头工作队队长许宏认为，如果将整个华夏族群比作一棵大树，二里头正是大树的主干，向上全是枝丫，因此，枝丫没有办法成为中国的代表。"最早的中国"成为河洛文化的一个重要标识。

最后，如果从文化延续的角度把中华文明的萌生、发展、兴盛过程概括为"文化中国"，把青铜时代以来自夏商周开启的二十五史演变称为"王朝中国"，那么，无论是"文化中国"还是"王朝中国"，分别以"河洛古国"和二里头遗址为代表，充分表明河洛文化是中华文化的源头与核心，是根文化、母文化和主流文化。

show tribe, community, or social status) were different. After the Qin and Han dynasties, *xing* and *shi* were integrated and they both became surnames that have continued to be used till this day. The hometown of the Yellow Emperor was in the Heluo region. According to the rough statistics of the descendants of the Yellow Emperor recorded in *Shiben(Book of Origins)*, Yellow Emperor had 25 sons and 12 of them bore the family name. From the time of Yellow Emperor to the pre-Qin period, the direct sub-clans of Yellow Emperor developed into 101 dependencies (vassal states) and 501 clans. The multiplication of the surnames by the descendants of Yellow Emperor constitutes an important part of the surnames of the Chinese nation today. According to statistics, more than 22,000 surnames have appeared in China since ancient times (at least 3,500 are still in use) including about two-thirds that originated in Henan Province.

Heluo culture, the root of Chinese civilization, is a powerful symbol of the earliest China. The original meaning of the word "China" refers to the Luoyang area. According to textual research, the word "China" first appeared in the inscription of the bronze ware He Zun made in the early Western Zhou Dynasty and unearthed in Baoji, Shaanxi Province, in 1965. The inscription "China" refers to the Chengzhou of the Zhou Dynasty, which overlaps with today's Luoyang area. As a result, Luoyang area was called Zhongtu (Middle Earth), and later Henan Province was also called Zhongzhou or Central Plains. If the entire Chinese ethnic group is compared to a big tree, Xu Hong, a researcher of Institute of Archaeology, Chinese Academy of Social Sciences and Director of Archaeology Research Office of Xia, Shang and Zhou Dynasties and Coordinator of the Erlitou Project, believes that Erlitou is the backbone of the big tree and is full of branches, so it is not a representative of China. The notion of the earliest China has become an important symbol of the Heluo culture.

Finally, from the perspective of cultural continuation, if the process of the initiation, development, and prosperity of Chinese civilization is summarized as "Cultural China," then the Bronze Age will be known as "Dynasty China" based on the evolution of 25 histories from the Xia, Shang and Zhou dynasties. Irrespective of whether it is "Cultural China" or "Dynasty China," it is represented by the Heluo Ancient Country and Erlitou Site respectively, a clear indication that the Heluo culture is the source and core culture, the root culture, the mother culture, and the mainstream culture of China.

第二章

古都文化

Chapter 2

Ancient Capital Culture

古都文化是指以古都为载体的历史文化。古都，作为王朝的政治文化中心，是一个王朝或一个时代重要的文化载体，呈现与代表着某一时期历史文明的最高水平。国内八大古都，河南就有洛阳、郑州、开封、安阳四个，形成了一个明显集中的古都群。特别是以洛阳为中心，夏、商、西周、东周、东汉、曹魏、西晋、北魏、隋、唐、后梁、后唐、后晋等13个朝代先后1500余年在这里建都，是我国建都年代最早、朝代最多、时间最长的古都。如果从中国历史独特的首都、陪都的双都制看，洛阳作为陪都还有新莽、东晋、南朝宋、后赵、东魏、北齐、北周、后汉、后周、北宋、金等11个朝代。

一、五都荟洛

中国有不少古都，在经历岁月沧桑后已经湮灭，难觅其踪。而洛阳千年帝都虽历经数次毁灭，但仍留存有大量的文化遗址使人凭吊与怀古。如今在沿洛河东西20多公里内分布的夏都斟鄩、商都西亳、周都成周与王城、汉魏故城、隋唐城遗址，以其"五都荟洛"的宏伟气魄见证着洛阳千年帝都的兴衰更替。

夏都斟鄩

洛阳是夏王朝的统治中心和都邑所在。二里头遗址在今偃师西南伊洛夹河之处，该遗址东西大约2千米，南北约1.5千米，总面积将近375万平方米。从发掘面积来看，内有宫城、宫殿、宗庙礼仪性建筑、祭祀性建筑、道路、各类房屋建筑、窖穴、灰坑、水井、墓葬群、青铜作坊、制骨作坊、陶窑等，还有大量的青铜器、玉器、陶器，文化层堆积丰厚，时间测定约在公元前1900—前1600年。这与文献记载斟鄩的方位、时间基本相吻合。二里头遗址产生了多项世界之最：最早的宫城，最早的中轴线布局的宫殿建筑群，最早的城市干道网，最早的青铜礼乐器群，最早的青铜近战兵器，最早的青铜器铸造作坊，最早的绿松石器

Ancient capital culture refers to the historical culture with the ancient capital as the carrier. The ancient capital, as the political and cultural center of a dynasty, epitomizes the most outstanding historical achievements during a particular period. Among the eight ancient capitals in China, four including Luoyang, Zhengzhou, Kaifeng, and Anyang are located in Henan creating a group of ancient capitals. Especially given its central position, Luoyang, for over a period of 1,500 years served as the capital of 13 dynasties including Xia (2070 BC-1600 BC), Shang (1600 BC-1046 BC), Western Zhou (1046 BC-771 BC), Eastern Zhou (770 BC-256 BC), Eastern Han (25 AD-220 AD), Cao Wei (220 AD-256 AD), Western Jin (266 AD-316 AD), Northern Wei (386 AD-534 AD), Sui (581 AD-618 AD), Tang (618 AD-907 AD), Later Liang (907 AD-923 AD), Later Tang (923 AD-936 AD), and Later Jin (936 AD-947 AD). Luoyang has the earliest history of building a capital city, the longest time of being the capital city, and the highest number of dynasties that had Luoyang as their capital. From the dual capital system perspective, that is, the capital and auxiliary capital system peculiar to China, Luoyang has served as the auxiliary capital of 11 dynasties including Xinmang (9 AD-23 AD), Eastern Jin (317 AD-420 AD), Liu Song of the Southern Dynasty (420 AD-479 AD), Later Zhao (319 AD-351 AD), Eastern Wei (534 AD-550 AD), Northern Qi (550 AD-557 AD), Northern Zhou (557 AD-581 AD), Later Han (947 AD-950 AD), Later Zhou (951 AD-960 AD), Northern Song (960AD-1127 AD), and Jin (1115AD-1234 AD).

I. Five Capital Sites in Luoyang

After experiencing vicissitudes, many ancient capitals in China have been annihilated and it is difficult to find their traces. Although Luoyang, the millennium imperial capital, was destroyed several times, there remain an impressive amount of cultural relics for people to probe and visit. Nowadays, Zhenxun, capital of the Xia Dynasty, Xibo of the Shang Dynasty, Chengzhou and Wangcheng of the Zhou Dynasty, city relics of the Han-Wei dynasties, and the capital relics of the Sui-Tang dynasties are located within more than 20 kilometers from east to west along the Luo River. These sites are testimony of the rise and fall of this ancient capital city.

作坊，最早的使用双轮车的证据，这里不愧为"最早的中国"。

图2-1 二里头遗址现场
Figure 2-1 Erlitou Site

偃师商城

商朝在成汤灭掉夏桀以后，把国都由亳（今河南商丘一带）迁到夏都斟鄩所在的河洛地区——西亳，即今偃师市区西的尸乡沟一带。史载："河南偃师为西亳，帝喾及汤所都，盘庚亦徙都之。"（《汉书·地理志》）1983年，中国社会科学院考古研究所在偃师县城（今偃师市区）西尸乡沟发现了这座遗址。商代的成汤、外丙、中壬、太甲、沃丁、太庚、小甲、雍已、太戊诸王，皆都西亳，总计偃师商城共历十三王，时间长达200余年。偃师商城遗址有大城和小城两重城墙，城墙外还设有护城河。以宫室为中心，周围分别建造有居住区、手工业作坊区、祭祀区、墓葬区等。从宫殿建筑基址看，已经具备了宫庙分离、对称布局、前朝后寝、内外有别的后世宫城的功能。偃师商城是商汤灭夏后所营建的早期都城，是迄今我国考古发现的商代早期城址中保存最好的一座城址。它的发现被联合国教科文组织列为1983年世界十七大发现之一。

Zhenxun, the capital of the Xia Dynasty

Luoyang represents the administrative center and the capital of the Xia Dynasty. Located in the southwest of the Yanshi City, the Erlitou site is sandwiched by the Yi river and Luo river. It extends 2km from the west to the east, 1.5km from the north to the south and it has a total surface area of 3.75 square meters. The excavation area comprises imperial courts, palaces, ancestral temples for sacrifice, buildings for sacrifice, paths, various residential architectures, cellars, ash pits, wells, tombs, bronze workshops, bone workshops, pottery kilns, etc. Also, there remain many cultural-loaded treasures including bronzes, jade, and pottery. It is believed that the cultural heritages were constructed between 1900 BC and 1600 BC, which almost coincides with the recorded location and time. The Erlitou site has been recognized as the earliest palace, the earliest palace clusters with a central axis layout, the earliest urban arterial network, the earliest bronze ritual musical instrument group, the earliest bronze melee weapon, the earliest bronze casting workshop, the earliest turquoise workshop, and the earliest evidence proving the use of two-wheeled vehicles. Therefore, it deserves recognition as "the earliest China".

Yanshi Shangcheng

After overthrowing the Xia Dynasty set up by Xia Jie, Cheng Tang, king of the Shang Dynasty (1600 BC-1046 BC) relocated the capital from Bo to Xibo in the Heluo region, the place where the capital of Xia—Zhenxun—lies, that is, today's Shixianggou in the west of Yanshi City. The "Geographical Records" chapter of *The Book of Han* documented that "Yanshi City in Henan Province used to be Xibo, the capital city chosen by Di Ku, Cheng Tang, and Pan Geng." The Chinese Academy of Social Science found this site in Shixianggou, west of Yanshi City, in 1983. Yanshi Shangcheng of the Shang Dynasty lasted for over 200 years and witnessed 13 kings totally including Cheng Tang, Wai Bing, Zhong Ren, Tai Jia, Wo Ding, Tai Geng, Xiao Jia, Yong Yi, and Tai Wu. Yanshi Shangcheng was surrounded by both tall and short city walls with a moat built outside the walls. At the center was the palace chamber, there are also residential houses, manufacturing workshops, sacrificial areas, and tombs. The palace boasted an outline of the characteristics of Chinese palaces that feature the separation of temples and palaces, the symmetrical layout, the front court, and rear chamber houses, as well as the distinct comparison between the inside and outside palace. Yanshi Shangcheng is

周都成周与王城

周代洛阳城的兴建是从周武王灭殷后营建洛邑开始的。西周时期的洛阳都城文献上一般称为"成周"。公元前770年，周平王正式东迁洛邑，拉开东周的序幕，其所居都城称为"王城"。从平王东迁到赧王五十九年（前256年）被秦昭王灭亡，风雨飘摇的东周在这545年的时间里，就是在洛阳定都的。考古发现，东周王城是一座面积巨大，四周有城墙、内城外廓布局的都城。东周王城西北部设有规模较大的作坊区，有制造陶器的窑场，也有制造石器、骨器、玉器的作坊，还有制造铜器的作坊。东周王城出土了大量东周时期的货币，足以证明当时东周王城商业的繁盛。

汉魏故城

西汉王朝建立，刘邦曾初都洛阳三个月，后在娄敬的劝说下迁都长安。西汉末年，王莽篡权，刘秀反击成功，在成周城遗址之上建立了东汉都城。公元220年，曹丕篡汉称帝，都洛阳。公元265年，晋武帝司马炎灭曹魏，西晋亦在洛阳建都。魏晋洛阳城在永嘉之乱后化为废墟。公元495年，北魏孝文帝将六宫及文武尽迁洛阳。汉魏故城是东汉、曹魏、西晋、北魏的都城遗址。其重要遗址有内城、外郭城城垣，东汉南北两宫、北魏太极殿、金墉城、北魏永宁寺、太学、辟雍、明堂、灵台、白马寺等。史载，公元166年，罗马帝国国王安敦派使者来到汉魏洛阳城，朝见汉桓帝，这是罗马与中国的第一次直接来往，标志着丝绸之路最东端与最西端直接交往的开始。罗马帝国与古代中国仅有4次交往，有3次都是来到了汉魏洛阳故城中，这座城市见证了中西方文化交往的开始以及丝绸之路第一次延伸到欧洲的过程。如今，汉魏故城作为丝绸之路的东方起点之一，再次架起了东西方文化交流的桥梁，促进世界"文化共同体"的建构与形成。

an early capital built after the Xia Dynasty and, based on archaeological excavations in China, is so far the best-preserved city site of the early Shang Dynasty. The site is listed as one of the seventeen great findings of 1983 by UNESCO.

Chengzhou and the "King City" of the Zhou Dynasty

The construction of Luoyang was not started until King Wu of the Zhou Dynasty overthrew the Shang Dynasty. Luoyang, the capital of the Western Zhou Dynasty is generally called "Cheng Zhou" in literature. In 770 BC, King Ping of the Zhou Dynasty ordered to move the capital eastwards. This was regarded as the beginning of the Eastern Zhou Dynasty whose capital was known as "King City." Since King Ping relocated the capital eastwards, the tottering Eastern Zhou Dynasty lasted for 545 years in Luoyang before King Zhao of the Qin state overthrew the regime. Archaeological findings indicate that "King City" was a huge capital city surrounded by city walls with a layout that featured an inner and outer city. There was a large-scale workshop area in northwest King City, including the kiln factories fabricating pottery and workshops making stone, bone, jade, and copper. Several copper coins of the Eastern Zhou Dynasty excavated in King City are evidence of the prosperity of that time.

City Relics of the Han-Wei Dynasties

After the founding of the Western Han Dynasty, Liu Bang selected Luoyang as the capital for three months before moving, under the persuasion of Lou Jing, to Chang'an. During the later years of the Western Han Dynasty, Wang Mang usurped the power while Liu Xiu succeeded in a counterattack that made him establish the capital of the Eastern Han Dynasty on the site of Chengzhou relics. In 220 AD, Cao Pi usurped the throne and established the capital in Luoyang. In 265 AD, Sima Yan, Emperor Wu of the Jin Dynasty, overthrew Cao Wei and established the Western Jin Dynasty with Luoyang as its capital. Luoyang City in the Wei and Jin Dynasties was reduced to ruins after the Yongjia Rebellion. In 495 AD, Emperor Wen of the Northern Wei Dynasty moved his cabinet and six palaces of the inner court to Luoyang. City relics of the Han-Wei dynasties include the Eastern Han, Cao Wei, Western Jin, and Northern Wei dynasties respectively. The important relics include the inner city, the outer city, the southern and northern palaces of the Eastern Han Dynasty, Taiji palace and Yongning Temple of the Northern Wei Dynasty, Jinyong city, Imperial College, Piyong, Mingtang, Lingtai,

图2-2　汉魏故城遗址考古发掘现场
Figure 2-2　Site of City Relics of the Han-Wei Dynasties

隋唐洛阳城

604年，隋炀帝继位，当年的十一月，他行幸洛阳，并下达了建造新洛阳城的诏书。隋唐洛阳城分为宫城、皇城、外廓城等，是我国中古时期规模宏大、气势壮观、名闻中外的一座大都会。唐高宗显庆二年（657年），高宗手诏改洛阳宫为东都。唐洛阳城，作为一座都城，虽然在地位上略低于西京长安城，但是，在有唐一代，因其与江左富庶之地位置接近和便利的漕运体系，成为唐代帝王经常的驻留之地。一代女皇武则天的大部分时间是在洛阳度过的，甚至在她登基的光宅元年（684年）将洛阳城改为"神都"，将洛阳的皇家禁苑西苑改为"神都苑"。洛阳神都的这一名号沿用到唐中宗神龙元年（705年），在这前后20余年的时间，洛阳成为事实上的京师之城。这一时期洛阳城中演绎的建筑大戏，如明堂、天堂的营造，都成为古代中国建筑史上颇有影响

and White Horse Temple. Historical records show that An Dun, emperor of the Roman Empire used to send ambassadors to Luoyang in the Han and Wei dynasties to meet Emperor Huan. These meetings symbolize the ever first communication between the Chinese and Roman authorities. It marks the direct contact between the easternmost and the westernmost countries along the Silk Road. Of the only four meetings that occurred between the two countries, three were held in Luoyang City which witnessed the beginning of the interaction between the east and the west cultures as well as the process through which the Silk Road was extended to Europe. Nowadays, city relics of the Han-Wei dynasties that also mark the eastern starting point of the Silk Road serve, for a second time, as the bridge to promote communication between the East and the West and to facilate the establishment of a "shared cultural community" for the world.

The Capital Relics of the Sui-Tang dynasties

In 604 AD, Emperor Yang of the Sui Dynasty succeeded to the throne. In November, he went to Luoyang and issued an edict to build a new Luoyang City. The capital relics of the Sui and Tang dynasties are composed of palaces, an imperial court, and outer cities that represent the grandiose large-scale metropolis city renowned both nationally and internationally in the middle ages. In 657 AD (the 2nd year of Xianqing period in the Tang Dynasty), Emperor Gao Zong wrote an in-person edict ordering that Luoyang be changed to the Eastern Capital. As a capital city, Luoyang was slightly lower than Chang'an City in terms of status in the Tang Dynasty, but it remained a frequent residence of emperors of the Tang Dynasty because it boasted a convenient water transportation system and adjoined the east of the Yangtze River considered wealthy land. When Empress Wu Zetian, whose reign title was Guang Zhai, was on the throne, she renamed Luoyang "Shendu" and the imperial garden–Xiyuan–as "Shenduyuan" in 684 AD, the first year of the Guangzhai years. The name Shendu was used until 705 AD, the first year of the Shenlong period and by this time, Luoyang had truly been the capital city for nearly 20 years. Several buildings were constructed at this time. They included Mingtang and Tiantang whose structure continued to have a significant influence on ancient Chinese architectural history. Unfortunately, the rebellion of An Lushan and Shi Siming brought turmoil and chaos to the city. After that, emperors in the Tang Dynasty seldom stayed in Luoyang until

的重大事件。安史之乱将洛阳拖进深重灾难之中,其后唐代皇帝就很少驻跸洛阳,直至唐昭宗在朱温的裹挟下东迁洛阳。后梁、后唐、后晋都以洛阳为帝都。隋唐洛阳城是隋唐两代的巍峨帝都。其布局独特,"洛水贯都,有河汉之象";皇城从东南西三面围宫城,"以象北辰藩卫";突破传统观念的非对称中轴线及其中轴线上气势壮观的标志性建筑群,充分体现了"天人合一"的设计理念。隋唐洛阳城作为我国古代都城营造的典范,不仅具有承前启后的作用,还对唐以后的都城及日本的平城京、平安京的设计产生了巨大的影响。

北宋时期,虽然京师在东京汴梁,洛阳仍称为西京,但这时的洛阳实质上已经不具备都城的地位与功能了。宋以后的洛阳,先是遭金人的战火蹂躏,后来又落入元人手中,日趋没落,到明清时期已经沦落为一座普通的地方城市了。

古都是人类历史璀璨文明的最高集成。从夏商周三代都城到汉魏、隋唐,洛阳古都文化不断形成、发展、演变,它在当时是支撑王朝与政权得以存在的内在精神支柱,也是国都乃至全国繁华兴盛的重要因素。洛阳古都,历经沧桑,几度兴衰,但历史文化从来不会远去,而是一直伴随着中华文明的成长与复兴。徘徊在洛河沿岸"五都荟洛"的遗址,既有"若问古今兴废事,请君只看洛阳城"的感慨,也满怀从古老历史走向新时代的豪迈。

Emperor Zhao Zong was threatened by Zhu Wen to move his capital eastward to Luoyang. The Later Liang, Later Tang, and Later Jin dynasties all chose Luoyang as their capital. The capital relics of the Sui-Tang dynasties were the magnificent capital during that time. Its unique layout is described as "Luo River runs through the capital like the Milky Way"; the imperial city surrounds the palace from the east, the west and the south guarded by the image of the northern star; the asymmetric central axis that breaks through the traditional concept and the spectacular architectures along the symmetric central axis fully embody the design concept of "harmony between man and nature." As a construction model of capitals in ancient China, Luoyang City in the Sui and Tang dynasties not only absorbed the architectural essence of former dynasties but also paved the way for dynasties that followed. What's more, it also had a huge impact on the design of Heijō-kyō and Heian-kyō in Japan.

Although the eastern capital Bianliang served as the capital during the Northern Song Dynasty, Luoyang continued to be called Xijing, the western capital, even though it no longer possessed the status and function of the capital. After the Song Dynasty, Luoyang was ravaged by Jin people in the war, then was captured by the Yuan people. These are the two factors that resulted in its decline. By the time of the Ming and Qing dynasties, it had become an ordinary local city.

Ancient capitals represent the outstanding achievements of brilliant civilizations in human history. From the capital of the Xia, Shang, and Zhou dynasties to that of the Han-Wei and Sui-Tang dynasties, Luoyang's ancient capital culture has lived on through its formation, development, and evolution. The culture was the spiritual backbone that sustained the dynasties and regimes, as well as the important factor that contributed to the development of its capital and the entire country. Luoyang, as a capital, experienced vicissitudes and rises and falls several times, but its history and culture have remained intact. Instead, Luoyang has accompanied the growth and revival of the Chinese civilization. A walk among the relics of The Gathering of Five Ancient Capitals Sites in Luoyang on the banks of Luo River indulges one with the emotion that the city has witnessed the rise and fall of Chinese history, and one may also feel the city striding towards the new era from its time-honored history.

二、帝都气象

"城市是伟大而至尊的。"对于"城池雄伟,宫苑壮丽,为天下之冠"的古都更是如此。阅读洛阳古都的文献记载,置身文化遗址的考古现场,观赏复建的文化景观,都能感受与遥想当年"文治煌煌,武功烈烈"的帝都气象。

帝都宫殿

班固曾在《东都赋》中描述过东汉洛阳都城,"增周旧,修洛邑,扇巍巍,显翼翼。光汉京于诸夏,总八方而为之极。是以皇城之内,宫室光明,阙庭神丽"。据《后汉书·百官志》记载,东汉洛阳宫城四面正门外筑有朱雀、玄武、青龙、白虎四阙。朱雀阙最为宏伟壮观。太极殿是汉魏洛阳城宫城正殿,是中国历史上第一座"建中立极"的宫城正殿,是中国历史上最大的正殿。太极殿的建造确定了汉魏洛阳城的建筑布局中心,由此确立的以太极殿为中心的单一宫城形制以及都城单一建筑轴线规制,以太极殿为大朝、东西堂两侧并列的"东西堂"制度,宫城三大主殿南北纵列的"五门三朝"制度,开创了中国古代宫室制度及都城布局的一个新时代。上阳宫是隋唐洛阳城的著名宫殿,高宗时修建,是高宗、武则天时期重要的宫廷政治活动场所。由于宫殿、门阙、台阁、亭观极尽豪奢,其负责营建的韦弘机,受到弹劾而免职。

帝都街道

汉魏故城最有名的街道是铜驼大街,它起自宫城正门阊阖门,一直延伸至洛阳城的正南门宣阳门,构成了城市的南北轴线。据说汉代以前的都城是没有轴线大街概念的,铜驼大街开创了我国古代都城轴线建筑的先例,是我国都城中最早的轴线大街。铜驼大街的来历源于此街两边高达3米的一对铜驼。骆驼是丝绸之路上物资交流运输的主要工具,寓意平安和富贵,从西汉起人们便开始铸造铜驼,将其视为圣物,它被

II. The Great Royal Capital

"Cities are great and respectable." This statement holds especially true for the ancient capital regarded as the crown of the whole country because of the majestic buildings and magnificent palaces. Readers do feel the atmosphere of the imperial court full of eminent offices and officials when they go through the records of the ancient capital, stand at the archaeological site of the cultural site, and visit the restored cultural landscape.

Imperial Palaces

In his article "Ode to Eastern Capitals", Ban Gu maintained that the capital of Luoyang during the Eastern Han Dynasty was "Rebuilt based on the Zhou Dynasty site, the capital is majestic. The new capital displays the achievements of the Han emperor to the world and served as a symbol of his rule. Within the royal city, the palaces were imposing, and other houses were also quite grand looking." According to *Book of the Later Han—Officials*, there stood four gates: Zhuque, Xuanwu, Qinglong, and Baihu, right outside the four facets of the palace. Of all these, Zhuque gate was the most magnificent. Taiji Palace was the main palace of all the imperial buildings of the Han-Wei dynasties. It was the first palace built at the center axis line and was also the largest main palace in Chinese history. The construction of Taiji Palace was determinant to the architectural center of Luoyang City in the Han-Wei dynasties. With Taiji Palace as the center, the unique palace principle and architectural axis regulation of the capital were established, which, combined with the eastern and western chambers system and the principle of the System of Five Gates and Three Places ushered in a new era in the principles and layout of the Chinese ancient palaces. Shangyang Palace was built during the reign of Emperor Gao Zong in the Tang Dynasty and was an important palace for political activities under the control of Emperor Gao Zong and Empress Wu. Wei Hongji, who was responsible for the construction, was impeached and removed for pouring money into the construction of the palaces, gates, and pavilions.

The Streets of the Capital

Tongtuo Street stretching from Changhe Gate, the front entrance of the

放置于北接皇宫、南连大市的中轴线上更是皇权的象征。铜驼大街一主两辅3道并行，共宽约40米，两侧对称布置有衙署和寺庙，商贾云集，寸土寸金。这里是楼苑台阁最密集的地方，也是诗酒逐欢、弦歌呕哑之处，充分表征着洛阳的富贵繁华。

帝都里坊

北魏洛阳城里坊布局环绕宫城。隋唐洛阳城的外郭城与皇城之间遍布里坊，为官吏私宅和百姓居住之地。隋有103坊，唐有109坊。里坊之间设市场，共三市。洛河南有二市：东为丰都市（唐改为南市），西为大同市（唐改为西市）。洛河北瀍河东岸为通远市（唐改为北市）。据开元元年（713年）的统计，洛阳居民有19万户，总人口数为118万。这一时期的洛阳应该是当时世界上规模最为宏大的城市之一。目前洛阳市正进行唐代明教坊、宁人坊、天街的"两坊一街"保护展示工程，通过坊墙、坊门、坊内十字街等遗址要素展示坊内格局，以呈现当时帝都的里坊景象。

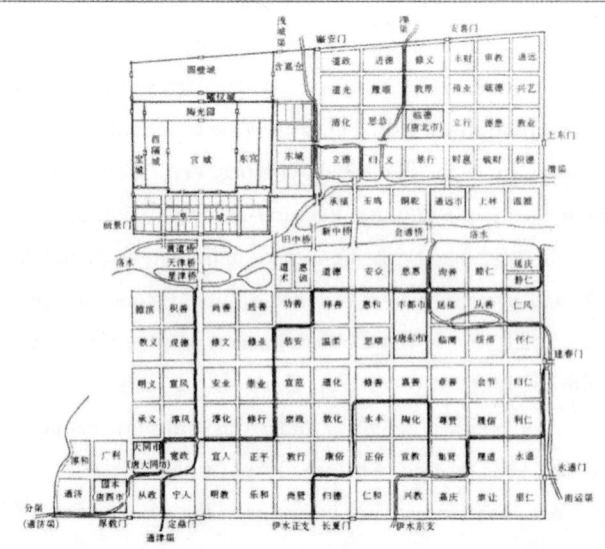

图2-3　隋唐洛阳里坊

Figure 2-3　Residential Houses in the Capital of Sui-Tang dynasties

court, to Xuanyang Gate, the south gate of Luoyang City, is the north-south axis of the city, and thus is renowned in the Han-Wei dynasties. It is said that capitals before the Han Dynasty did not have the axis street concept. Tongtuo Street was the precedent for the axis architecture, as well as the earliest axis street of capitals in ancient China. The name Tongtuo Street comes from a pair of copper camels that are 3 meters high on both sides of this street. Symbolizing safety and wealth, camels were the main tool for trade on the Silk Road. People from the Western Han Dynasty began to cast bronze camels and regarded them as sacred objects which were placed on the central axis as the symbol of imperial power. Tongtuo Street had one main and two auxiliary parallel lanes that had a total width of about 40 meters. Across the streets were government offices and temples symmetrically arranged on both sides, numerous merchants trading in the prosperous but high-price land. The place boasted most of the towers, gardens, and pavilions, and it is also the place where literates gathered for entertainment during which they created poems, drank wine, and played instruments. Their actions, it should be noted, fully represented the prosperity of Luoyang.

Residential Area in the Capital City

Residential areas surrounded the imperial court during the Northern Wei Dynasty. In the Sui and Tang dynasties, the outer city and the imperial city were covered with residential houses the majority of which were private residences of officials and ordinary people's houses. There were 103 and 109 alleys in the Sui and Tang dynasties respectively with a total of three markets. There were two markets in the south of Luo River: Fengdu Market in the east (renamed Nanshi in the Tang Dynasty) and Datong Market in the west (also renamed Xishi). Tongyuan Market (later called Beishi) was located between the north bank of Luo River and the east bank of Chan River. According to statistics of the first year of Kaiyuan (713), Luoyang had 190,000 households with a total population of 1.18 million, so it was one of the largest cities in the world at that time. At present, Luoyang City is carrying out the Two lanes and One Street protection display project in the Mingjiao area, Ningren area, and Tian Street that existed during the Tang Dynasty. To represent the residential areas in the capital at that time, the layout is shown through essential relics including the walls, gates, and cross streets in the area.

帝都园林

在洛阳建都的历代帝王也都倾心于园林苑囿。曹魏时期魏文帝建筑了西游园：园中有凌云台，台上有八角井，台下有碧海曲池。北魏时期的华林园，《洛阳伽蓝记》记载：华林园中有大海，即汉天渊池。池中犹有（魏）文帝九华台。高祖于台上造清凉殿，世宗在海内作蓬莱山，山上有仙人馆。（台）上有钓台殿，并作虹蜺阁，乘虚来往。此外，华林园中还豢养有波斯国王进献的狮子，以及巩县（今巩义市）、山阳所献的虎、豹、熊等动物。隋唐时期是洛阳园林营造的高峰时期。隋初隋炀帝在洛阳城西建造了"西苑"，《隋书·食货志》载：苑囿连接，北到新安，南及飞山，西至渑池，周围数百里。这是一座以建筑景观为特点的大型园林，园中有一条蜿蜒曲折的水渠，称"龙鳞渠"，在曲渠的每一个弯折之间，布置一座可供居住的院落，其内共造十六院，庭植名花，四面郁茂。西苑继承了西汉长安太液池"一池三山"的传统，苑内有方丈、蓬莱、瀛洲诸山，山高出水百余尺。风亭月观，皆以机成。据《大业杂记》记载：湖中积土石为山，构亭殿，屈曲环绕澄澈，皆穷极人间华丽。西苑是一座以水景为主、以建筑为主要造景元素的大型园林，其建筑物本身既是园林中的重要景观，也是可供起居生活的空间，这为后世具有离宫性质的清代皇家园林所发扬光大。除了皇家御园之外，汉唐名臣勋贵在洛阳也建有名园。西晋时以奢侈而著称的石崇，其"金谷园"在潘岳《金谷诗》中有所描述：园内瀑布飞流，湖光山色，果林成片，亭台华美，地势崎岖，曲径通幽。

最能代表帝都气象的是隋唐洛阳城中轴线上的"七天"建筑。隋唐洛阳城中轴线的确定源自于隋炀帝。公元604年十一月，隋炀帝东巡洛阳，他登上北邙山的翠云峰，向南极目远眺伊阙，但见两山对峙，伊水中流，气象非凡，遂顾左右而言道："此非龙门耶？自古何因不建都于此？"于是帝都的中轴线确立，伊阙也从此又称"龙门"。经过隋唐两代的不断建设，到武则天的"大周"时期，洛阳"神都"中轴线

Gardens of the Capital

Emperors who had their capitals in Luoyang were fond of building gardens. During the Cao-Wei period, Emperor Wen built Xiyou Garden in which there stood Lingyun pavilion on which was Bajiao Well (an octagonal well) and under which was Bihai Quchi. According to the *Record of Buddhist Temples in Luoyang*, the Hualin garden in the Northern Wei Dynasty housed a pond known later in the Han Dynasty as the Tianyuan pond. There also stood Jiuhua pavilion built during the reign of Emperor Wen in the Wei Dynasty. Liubang, whose posthumous title is Emperor GaoZu, built Qingliang Palace on the pavilion while Liu Che, also known as Emperor Wu in the Han Dynasty, ordered the building of a rockery called Penglai above which was Xianren Palace. On the pavilion, there was Diaotai Palace, that is, the Hongni Palace that was visited by an endless stream of people. In addition, Hualin Garden also housed lions donated by the king of Persia, tigers, leopards, bears, and other animals sent from Gongxian county and Shanyang county. The Sui and Tang dynasties represented the prime period in constructing gardens in Luoyang. During the early Sui Dynasty, Emperor Yang built Xiyuan garden in western Luoyang City. *The Book of Sui · Shihuo Record* documented that the garden covered an area of nearly a hundred square meters stretching to Xin'an county in the north, Feishan county in the south, and Mianchi county in the west. It was a large-scale garden characterized by its architecture and through which ran a winding stream called Longlinqu. Between each bend of the stream, a courtyard was constructed for living. There were a total of sixteen houses surrounded by famous flowers and lush vegetation. The construction of Xiyuan garden inherited the tradition of one pool with three mountains left by the Taiye pool in Chan'an City during the Western Han Dynasty. Rockeries like Fangzhang, Penglai, and Yingzhou were built over 100 feet above the water. The garden provided people with the opportunity to appreciate the attractive landscape. According to the *Miscellaneous Records of the Great Cause*: "Piled up the earth and rocks dug out from the lake, there were rockeries or even pavilions surrounded by streams, all of which were exceedingly gorgeous on earth." Xiyuan is a large garden with a waterscape with its theme and architecture the main landscaping element. The buildings themselves are not only important landscape in the garden but also living spaces. These features were

上汇聚了蔚为壮观的"七天建筑群",从北到南依次为:天堂、天宫(明堂)、天门(应天门)、天枢、天津(天津桥)、天街、天阙(伊阙)。天堂,始建于公元689年,是一代女皇武则天感应四时、与天沟通的礼佛堂。明堂,据记载:高二百九十四尺,东西南北各广三百尺。凡有三层,下层象四时,各随方色。中层法十二辰。圆盖,盖上盘九龙捧之。上层法二十四气,亦圆盖。亭中有巨木十围,上下通贯。应天门,为宫城的正南门,其在都城中最为尊崇,若元正、冬至、陈乐、宴会、赦宥罪、除旧布新,当万国朝贡使者、四夷宾客等重要庆典,皇帝均登临听政。开元二十一年(733年),唐玄宗在此接见日本第八次"遣唐使"。应天门是一组由门楼、朵楼、阙楼及其相互之间的廊庑连为一体的巨大建筑群,双向三出阙,两侧共六阙,是中国古代宫城正门的最高礼制,这种建筑形制对北宋、明清的都城建筑影响深远。

图2-4　隋唐应天门复建图
Figure 2-4　Image of Yingtian Gate in Sui andTang dynasties

天枢,位于宫城外,为武则天所铸的歌功颂德纪念碑。天枢高约31.06米,上面除了武则天自书的"大周万国颂德天枢",柱身还刻有大唐文武百官和各国首领的名字。天津(天津桥),位于洛水之上。史

continued in palaces built during the Qing Dynasty. In addition to the imperial gardens, famous officials and royal relatives in the Han and Tang dynasties also built gardens in Luoyang that were popular in later generations. In the Western Jin Dynasty, an officer called Shi Chong, known for his luxurious living style, possessed a garden named Jingu garden. Pan Yue described the garden in his book *Jingu Poem* as follows: "The waterfall plunges to water; lakes and hills create a picturesque landscape, with a large area of fruit trees planted around; gorgeous pavilions are built in the garden; the rugged while winding path leads to a tranquil and serene place."

Qitian Buildings on the central axis of Luoyang City were representative of the imperial court in the Sui and Tang dynasties. The central axis of Luoyang City originated from Emperor Yang of the Sui Dynasty. In November 604 AD, Emperor Yang made a tour eastwards of Luoyang. When he ascended Cuiyun Peak of the north Mang mountain, he looked southwards to Yique county. Seeing the two mountains standing opposite between which flew the Yi River, the emperor was astonished by this extraordinary scene and said, "Isn't it the symbol of the true son of Heaven? Why has there been no capital here since ancient time?" This is how the central axis of the imperial capital was determined, and Yique, from then on, was also renamed Longmen. Through endless construction during the Sui and Tang dynasties, the spectacular Qitian Buildings were completed on the central axis in Luoyang in the Wu Zhou Dynasty established by Wu Zetian. From north to south, the buildings were Heavenly Hall, Tiangong (Hall of Enlightment), Tianmen (Yingtian Gate), Tianshu, Tianjin (Tianjin Bridge), Tianjie, and Tianque (Yique) respectively. Heavenly Hall, constructed in 689 AD, was a hall that Empress Wu Zetian used for praying for God and worshipping Buddha. The Hall of Enlightenment was two hundred and ninety-four feet high, and its radius was three hundred feet. It was a three-story building with the ground floor representing the four seasons, each with its distinctive color; the second floor indicating the 12 two-hour periods of a day with a round cover along the external side, and on the cover squatted nine dragons. The top floor represented the 24 solar terms and also had a round cover. In the middle of the building stood a huge column right to the roof. Yingtian Gate, the south front gate of the palace, was the most respected in the capital because the emperor

料记载唐高宗到东都时,百官曾到天津桥南迎接。"天津晓月"是洛阳"八大景"之一。天街即定鼎门大街,为全城的南北中轴大街。天阙即伊阙、龙门,是洛阳南面的天然门户,两岸高山对立,中有江水流动,远望仿佛天然且宏伟的门阙。具有标志性的"七天"建筑群,是我国古代最豪华壮观的都城中轴线,可谓独一无二。联想大唐有容乃大,万国之人纷纷前来,身处城内猛然看到体量巨大、气势恢宏的"七天"景观,其震撼与崇敬实在难以想象。

图2-5　洛阳丽景门　刘龙/摄
Figure 2-5　Lijing Gate, Luoyang　Photo by Liu Long

used to ascend the gate to handle affairs including meeting ambassadors and guests from the neighboring countries, celebrating festivals, and issuing decrees. In the 21st year of the Kaiyuan reign (year 733), Emperor XuanZong of the Tang Dynasty met the eighth Japanese envoys at this place. Yingtian Gate was a huge building complex consisting of gateways, Duo towers (annex building beside the main building on both sides), gate towers, and the veranda which connected the above three buildings. The whole building had three gate towers on each side, and six gate towers in total. It was the highest ritual system of the main gate of ancient Chinese palaces. This architectural form had a profound impact on the capital architecture of the Northern Song Dynasty, Ming, and Qing dynasties.

Tianshu, located outside the palace, is a monument to Wu Zetian's eulogy. It is 31.06 meters high and on the column is engraved "Tianshu, the monument for praising the virtue around the country." Also, the name of officials of the dynasty and leaders of all countries are engraved on it. Tianjin (Tianjin Bridge) was constructed across the Luo River. According to historical documents, when Emperor GaoZong of the Tang Dynasty arrived in the eastern capital, officials and officers went to the south of Tianjin bridge to meet him. Tianjin Xiaoyue is one of the eight great sights in Luoyang. Tianjie is the so-called Dingdingmen street, which is the central axis connecting the south and the north of the city. Tianque is also called Yique and Longmen is the natural gateway to the south of Luoyang. There are opposite mountains on both sides of the bank with the river that is flowing through looking like a natural and magnificent gate from a far distance. The iconic and unique Qitian architectural complex is the most luxurious and magnificent central axis in ancient times. It is hard to imagine the surprise and respect of foreigners when they came and saw the huge and magnificent Qitian Buildings in this inclusive city.

三、帝陵森然

洛阳帝陵与洛阳古都密切相关，是其古都文化的重要载体。帝王将相是古都舞台的风云人物，他们生前的尊崇与荣耀在中国人"视死如生"的观念支配下必然也要体现在陵墓建筑之中。如今在洛阳周围，分布着数百座高大巍峨、森然壮观的墓冢。特别是城市北边的邙山，从汉代到唐代，一直是人们向往的长眠之地，达官贵人、富商巨贾都以能得到邙山一块墓地而自豪。"北邙山头少闲土，尽是洛阳人旧墓"，唐朝诗人王建的一句诗写出了邙山的"寸土寸金"和生命的拥挤。"富贵至今何处是，断碑零碎野人耕。"（薛瑄《北邙行》）登临邙山，在星罗棋布、各具特色的古墓间穿行，既隐现着洛阳城与墓主人远去的光荣，也感受到杂草和荆棘之间的晚风凄凉。那显示荣耀的祭殿和道碑，或残留农舍，或荡然无存。"北邙山上列坟茔，万古千秋对洛城。"（沈佺期《邙山》）洛阳帝都与邙山，构成一个巨大的"生死场"，"北邙"居高临下地俯视着滚滚红尘的洛阳城，使城中的歌舞狂欢与山上的松柏森然有趣地拼贴，它们之间既有着生与死的富贵延续，也有着阴阳两界的抵牾拆解，生与死的对话使"洛阳八大景"之一的"邙山晚眺"别具文化意味。

"生居苏杭，死葬北邙。"北邙也即邙山，是崤山向东延伸的余脉。从古代堪舆学讲，邙山南系悠悠洛水，北临滔滔黄河，面向苍苍嵩岳，背负巍巍太行，大势上看是典型的避风聚水之地，符合"枕山蹬河"的葬俗，是阴宅的"首善之区"。东晋诗人陶渊明诗云："一旦百岁后，相归于北邙。"据考察，邙山古墓葬分布之密堪称"无卧牛之地"。冢连冢、墓压墓，墓葬数量之多、年代之久，堪称中国之最。等级分明的墓葬、密集的墓葬群、价值连城的陪葬品，使北邙有"东方金字塔"之称。

III. Majestic Tombs

Imperial mausoleum in Luoyang are closely related to the ancient capital and it serves as an important carrier of its ancient capital culture. The emperors, officers, and officials were the influential figures of the ancient capital, so the respect and glory during their lifetime were inevitably reflected in the mausoleum in accordance with the long-standing Chinese philosophy that considers death as great as life. Today, there are hundreds of tall, majestic tombs around Luoyang particularly on Mount Mang in the north of the city that has been the most desired burial place for people from the Han Dynasty to the Tang Dynasty. Dignified officials and wealthy merchants are proud to be buried in Mount Mang. Wang Jian, a poet of the Tang Dynasty remarked in his poem that "Not a piece of land is vacant on Mangshan because of the full occupation of Luoyang people's tombs", reflecting how many tombs were there and how precious they were in Mount Mang. "Where are the riches and honors of long ago? Broken tombstones are now in the farming fields" (Xue Xuan's poem "Travel to Beimang Mountain"). While climbing Mount Mang and walking among the distinctive ancient tombs, it is possible to notice the past glory of Luoyang City and those buried there, and feel the desolation as weeds and thorns sway in the wind in the evening. The temples where sacrifices were conducted as well as monuments displaying glory were either used for farming or were completely ruined. "Mount Mang is filled with tombs which have faced Luoyang City for thousands of years" (Shen Quanqi's poem "Mount Mang"). The capital and Mount Mang make a distinctive contrast, that is, the field of life and death. Mount Mang condescendingly overlooks the prosperous and living city—a city that boasts feasts and forests outside the city complementing with each other. There is the continuation of wealth and honor between life and death, as well as the conflict and dismantling of the yin and yang. The contrast between life and death makes the "Evening Landscape in Mount Mang", one of the "eight great sceneries in Luoyang", reflect its unique culture.

"To live in the paradise of Suzhou and Hangzhou and be buried in Mount Mang." Mount Mang is the eastern branch of Mount Xiao. According to

帝陵是洛阳邙山陵墓群的主体。据统计，邙山陵墓群总数在千座以上，陵墓群包括东周、东汉、曹魏、西晋、北魏、后唐等6朝24座帝王陵墓及其陪葬墓群，其中东周王墓8座，东汉帝陵5座，曹魏帝陵1座，西晋帝陵5座，北魏帝陵4座，五代后唐帝陵1座。这些帝王，有的在历史上曾叱咤风云，其中有大名鼎鼎的东汉开国皇帝光武帝刘秀，以迁都促进民族大融合而青史留名的北魏孝文帝，也有的一闪而过，仅在历史中留下一个模糊的背影，如汉冲帝刘炳，他2岁即位，3岁即崩，在位还不到一年。从墓葬考古看，曹魏、西晋帝陵依山为体，无封土；东汉、北魏陵区现存地面封土尚有300多座，呈覆斗形或圆锥形，最大者直径在100米以上，高50余米。出土的大量墓志，内容涉及政治、经济、军事、文化、中外交往、民族关系等，为历史研究提供了重要的资料。邙山陵墓群是目前中国面积较大的国家文物保护单位，也是世界上古代陵墓分布较为集中的地区之一。

东周王陵"天子驾六"的横空出世，见证了2000多年前周王室的威仪。《逸礼·王度记》记载：天子驾六，诸侯驾四，士驾二。即在周代，车马是主人等级身份的象征，普天之下只有天子才可以乘坐六匹马拉的车。但时序推移到了东汉，许慎、郑玄却为周天子"驾六"或是"驾四"发生了激烈争论。这场发生在公元2世纪的关于古制天子驾数的经学争论，大约历经了1800多年悠悠岁月的等待，在2002年年底才最终尘埃落定。当年在洛阳东周王城遗址上，发现一处东周时期的大型墓地及车马坑群。在规模最大的车马坑内其中一辆马车前，发现了对称摆放着的6匹马的骨骸，这"驾六马"的"天子之乘"以直观清晰的形式，向世人印证了古文献中"天子驾六"的记述。虽然过了近3000年，车辕、车身的构件及马的骨骼仍清晰可见。"天子驾六"保存完好，规模宏大，再现了东周时期的乘舆制度、丧葬文化。

ancient geomancy, Mount Mang adjoins the Luo River in the south and the surging Yellow River in the north, and it also faces Mount Song at the front and Mount Taihang at the back. A simple glimpse indicates how the place is typical, abundant with water that shelters the wind, and conforms to the burial custom "with mountains as pillows and rivers at the feet" which is the most solicited tomb type by the people. Tao Yuanming, a poet of the Eastern Jin Dynasty, once said, "The dead are buried in north Mang mountain when they pass by." According to research, tombs in Mount Mang are so close to each other that there is no room left for a cow to lie. The mountain, filled with tombs, is regarded as the most ancient burial ground. It is known as the "Pyramid of the East" because of its hierarchical system, dense tomb groups, and priceless funerary objects.

Imperial mausoleums are a prominent feature of Mount Mang tombs in Luoyang. According to statistics, there are more than a thousand tomb groups on Mount Mang including 24 imperial tombs and their attendant tombs spreading over 6 dynasties including Eastern Zhou, Eastern Han, Cao-Wei, Western Jin, Northern Wei, and Later Tang dynasties and accounting for 8, 5, 1, 5, 4 and 1 tomb respectively. Historically, some of these were successful and powerful emperors including Liu Xiu, also known as Emperor Guang Wu, the founder of the Eastern Han Dynasty, and Emperor Xiao Wen of the Northern Wei Dynasty, whose relocation of the capital promoted national integration and became famous in history. Some of the emperors died early, so they did not have the opportunity to realize their ambitions. For example, Liu Bing (Emperor Chong) of the Han Dynasty, who took the throne at the age of 2 and deceased at the age of 3, reigned for less than a year. From the perspective of tomb archaeology, the tombs of the Cao-Wei and Western Jin dynasties were built on the mountain without a mound of earth over them. By contrast, there are more than 300 mounds built in the Eastern Han and Northern Wei that still exist and are shaped like an overturned bucket or cone with the largest over 100 meters in diameter and over 50 meters in high. Inscriptions on the memorial tablet of a tomb cover the economy and military as well as culture, Sino-foreign communication, ethnic relations, etc., providing important data for historical research. The tomb group on Mount Mang is, currently, a large national cultural relic reserve in China, and it is also one of the areas with the largest concentration of ancient tombs in the world.

图2-6　天子驾六车马坑
Figure 2-6　Pit of Emperor's Six-horse Chariot

　　历代王侯将相、达官贵人以葬于北邙为荣。帝陵周围还长眠着自东周一直到明清各朝代数不胜数的王侯将相、才士名流。现存有秦相吕不韦、南朝陈后主、南唐李后主、唐朝诗人杜甫、大书法家颜真卿等历代名人之墓。甚至还有从丝绸之路过来的"外国人"安息在洛阳城北这几十里的土岭上。邙山古墓中长眠的人，都曾目睹洛阳城的辉煌与沧桑。

　　灿若繁星的洛阳古墓群，成为千年帝都丰厚的历史文化遗存，形成一道古朴厚重的人文景观。洛阳出土的珍贵文物数不胜数。国内外许多博物馆的镇馆之宝出自洛阳的邙山。伴随着各种出土的文物，尘封久远的古老文明在洛阳被慢慢地揭开了神秘的面纱。虽然今天的邙山土岭上

More than 2000 years ago, an ancient etiquette required the emperor to enjoy a six-horse chariot. According to *Wangduji*, "The emperor is entitled to enjoy a six-horse chariot, ministers a four-horse chariot, and warriors a two-horse chariot." Chariots and horses symbolized the status of master during the Zhou Dynasty, and only the emperor had the right to enjoy a six-horse horse chariot around the whole territory. However, Xu Shen and Zheng Xuan in the Han Dynasty had a fierce dispute over whether the emperors during the Zhou Dynasty enjoyed a six- or four-horse chariot. The debate about the horse number was in the second century AD and was finally settled about 1,800 years later at the end of 2002 when in a large cemetery, a group of cart and horse pits belonging to the Eastern Zhou Dynasty was unearthed on the site of the Wangcheng relics. The skeletons of six horses were found placed symmetrically in front of a chariot in the largest scale chariot and horse pit. This discovery proved the recording of the emperor's unique six-horse chariot. Although nearly 3,000 years had passed, the shaft and body of the chariot, along with the skeleton of horse bones were still clearly visible. The emperor's six-horse chariot was well-reserved with a grand scale, showing the vehicle system and funeral culture of the Eastern Zhou Dynasty.

Royal families, high officers, and noble lords were proud to be buried in north Mang mountain. From the Eastern Zhou Dynasty to the Ming and Qing dynasties, countless princes, noble lords, and celebrities were buried around the imperial mausoleum. The existing tombs belong to Lv Buwei, the prime minister of the Qin Dynasty, Chen Shubao, the last emperor of the Southern Dynasty, Li Yu, the last emperor of the Southern Tang Dynasty, Du Fu, the famous poet of the Tang Dynasty, and Yan Zhenqing, the well-known calligrapher. There were even foreigners who came to China along the Silk Road who slept peacefully in this final resting place. All the people buried here had witnessed the glory and vicissitudes of Luoyang City.

Countless mausoleum groups in Luoyang have formed profound historical and cultural relics in this millennium capital city providing a time-honored cultural landscape. Precious cultural relics unearthed in Luoyang are exceedingly numerous and these treasures that are now in numerous museums both at home and abroad were uncovered in Mount Mang in Luoyang City. With the

图2-7 天子驾六雕塑

Figure 2-7 Museum of Emperor's Six-horse Chariot

已经看不到当年大片的郁郁青松,但草木萋萋的北邙仍不失其雄浑与肃穆,那古墓冢上的杂草和荆棘在风中猎猎作响,似乎在诉说着早已远去的历史荣光。

图2-8 隋唐定鼎门（局部）
Figure 2-8 Dingding Gate of Sui and Tang Dynasties (Part)

unearthing of various cultural relics, the history of ancient Chinese civilization has gradually been exposed in Luoyang. The landscape of lush pines on Mount Mang has faded away, but the mountain, covered with luxuriant vegetation, still looks grand and sepulchral. Thorns and weeds on the tombs are rustle in the breeze as if they are murmuring the historical glory that has gone with the wind.

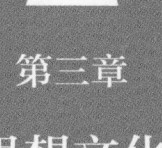

第三章

思想文化

Chapter 3

Ideology and Culture

河洛思想文化主要是指在河洛地区形成的思想文化，河洛思想文化是河洛文化的重要组成部分，其形成、发展与河洛"千年帝都"的历史密不可分，并成为中央文化、国家文化、国都文化、统治文化。举其要者，儒学起源于洛阳，道教创始于洛阳，佛教首传于洛阳，玄学兴盛于洛阳，理学光大于洛阳。这五大思想流派具有源发性、正统性、主导性，其对中华民族人文思想和品格的形成影响深远，从某种意义上甚至决定了中国历史的走向。

一、河洛儒学

　　周公在洛阳制礼作乐。礼的主要内容包括宗法制、封诸侯、五服制，爵位、谥法、官制、刑法，以及吉（祭祀）、凶（丧葬）、军（检阅、出征）、宾（朝觐、述职）、嘉（婚礼）五礼等。乐，是为配合上述典礼仪式而举行的乐舞。周公把《大韶》及《云门》《大章》《大夏》《大武》等加工整理，订为"六代乐舞"。西周的礼制保存在《周礼》《仪礼》《礼记》三部书中，号称《三礼》。周公制礼作乐，以嫡长子继承制、分封制、宗法制等为代表，对各阶层确定坐标，做出约束，防止其超越名分，从而维护社会秩序。这是夏商以来中国思想从敬鬼神到重人事的一大转变，对儒家仁义学说产生巨大影响。由于周公对儒家学说的贡献，故被后世称为儒家思想的奠基者，并被誉为"元圣""儒宗"。洛阳是周公制礼作乐的地方，因此又称为儒教祖庭。周公的礼乐思想影响中国数千年，是河洛文化的一座丰碑。

　　孔子"入周问礼"。孔子被称为儒家的"至圣"。孔子十分赞赏周公，由此非常向往周文化，曾说："郁郁乎文哉，吾从周。"孔子因倾慕西周盛世，便于周景王二十四年（前521年）到东周王都洛阳考查"礼乐之原"。在洛阳，他"问礼于老子，访乐于苌弘"，以考"礼乐之极"。《史记》记载：孔子适周问礼于老子。老子曰："君子得其时

The Heluo ideological culture mainly refers to the culture formed in the Heluo region. Ideological culture is one of the most important parts of Heluo culture, and its development is closely related to the history of the millennium imperial capital in the Heluo region. It has become the central culture, national culture, capital culture, and ruling culture. In a word, it was in Luoyang that Confucianism was initiated, Taoism started, Buddhism initially preached, Metaphysics flourished, and Neo-Confucianism prospered. Based on their origin, orthodoxy, and dominance, these five ideological cultures have had a profound influence on Chinese humanistic ideology and personality, and, to a certain extent, have even determined Chinese history.

I. Confucianism in the Heluo Region

According to historical records, Jidan, the Duke of Zhou, created a system of rites and music in Luoyang. The rites mostly included a patriarchal clan system, vassal system, Wufu system, regulations for posthumous titles, official system, criminal law, and the five ceremonies: auspicious (sacrifice), inauspicious (funeral), military (parade and expedition), guest (audience and debriefing), and fine (wedding). Music refers to the music and dance performed in the above ceremonies. Works including *Da Shao*, *Yun Men*, *Da Zhang*, *Da Xia* and *Da Wu* were reorganized by the Duke of Zhou into a new work known as Six Generations of Music and Dance. Three books of *Zhou Li*, *Yi Li*, and *Li Ji*, known as *The Three Rites*, preserved the system of rites and music of the Western Zhou Dynasty (1046 BC-771 BC). Represented by the primogeniture system, the feudal system, and the patriarchal clan system, the system of rites and music regulated the behavior of every social stratum and, as a way of maintaining the feudal order, restrained them from going beyond their stratum. This was a great shift that took place in Chinese philosophy from worshiping the spirits to valuing human beings beginning from the Xia and Shang dynasties and which had a significant impact on the Confucian doctrine of benevolence and righteousness. The Duke of Zhou was called the founder of Confucianism and was praised as the Supreme Sage and Confucian Ancestor by the later generations because of his contribution to Confucianism. It is in Luoyang that the system of rites and music

则驾,不得其时则蓬累而行。吾闻之,良贾深藏若虚,君子盛德,容貌若愚。"此外,孔子还瞻仰了周室先王太庙,见到那里的"金人"。《孔子家语》称他曾"历郊社之所,考明堂之则,察庙朝之度";孔子"观乎明堂,睹四门墉有尧舜之容、桀纣之象,而各有善恶之状、兴废之诫焉。又周公相成王,抱之负斧扆,南面以朝诸侯之图焉,孔子徘徊望之,谓从者曰:'吾今乃知周公之圣与周所以王也'"。在今洛阳市老城东关大街,保存着石碑一通,正面书写"孔子入周问礼乐至此"九个大字,由清代雍正年间河南知府张汉书,洛阳县令郭朝鼎刻立。孔子是儒家思想集大成者,"入周问礼"表明孔子的思想来源于周公,而周公的思想形成于在洛阳执政时期,因此,儒家学说根在河洛。

图3-1 孔子入周问礼处

Figure 3-1 The Site of Confucius Consulting Lao Zi for Rituals of Zhou

was established, so that is why Luoyang is also also known as the ancestral court of Confucianism. As a symbol of the Heluo culture, the rituals of Zhou have influenced China for thousands of years.

Confucius, known as the Supreme Holy of Confucianism, arrived in Luoyang in the Zhou Dynasty to find out the true system of rites and music. He was deeply attracted by the Zhou's culture because he had immense admiration for the Duke of Zhou. He once said, "Of all the cultures, I prefer that of Zhou." According to historical records, Confucius admired the prosperity of the Western Zhou Dynasty. So, in the 24th year of Emperor Jing of the Zhou Dynasty (521 BC), he left for the capital of the Eastern Zhou Dynasty, Luoyang, and visited "the origin of rituals of Zhou." He consulted Lao Tzu about rites, and Changhong about music to find the real system of rites and music in Luoyang. *The Records of the Historian* claims that Confucius arrived at the state of Zhou and learned rituals from Lao Tzu. Lao Tzu told him, A man of virtue waits in the wings to seize the opportunity, otherwise, he roams randomly. And I heard that a good merchant or businessman will hide his treasure and pretend to be poor rather than show off; a man of virtue looks very dull but with a great virtue in his heart. In addition, Confucius visited the ancestral temple of the former emperors of the Zhou Dynasty and saw the "copperman" in Luoyang. *The Confucian School's Analects* maintain, "Confucius worshiped the sites of sacrifice to the heaven and earth, investigated the rules of Ming Hall, and learned the system of the ancestral temple and the imperial hall…On the city walls, Confucius saw the portraits of Yao Emperor, Shun Emperor, Emperor Jie and Emperor Zhou with warnings about the rise and fall of their countries…There was also a portrait of the Duke of Zhou holding Emperor Cheng, the child emperor, in his arms and facing southwards towards Pingfeng to receive the hajj from the feudal lords, who assisted Emperor Cheng." Confucius wandered around and looked at the portraits one by one, then said to his followers, "This is the reason why the Duke of Zhou is so wise and the Zhou Dynasty flourished." There is a stele on Dongguan Street, Laocheng District in Luoyang on the front of which are inscribed nine Chinese characters, "Site Where Confucius Consulted the Rituals of Zhou," that was erected by Zhang Hanshu and Guo Chaoding during the Emperor Yongzheng period of the Qing Dynasty. The former was a governor of Henan Province,

东汉河洛地区经学繁盛。曾是太学生的东汉开国皇帝刘秀对儒学及儒术很感兴趣，在创建东汉王朝的过程中，刘秀"爱好经术，未及下车，而先访儒雅，采求阙文，补缀漏逸"。东汉建立后，刘秀又召集四方儒者，建立太学。他的儿子汉明帝更按照儒家的礼仪制度，冀望通过施行儒家所尊奉的仪式，来取得嗣位的合法性与权威性。他还亲自登场，召集儒生来讨论儒家经典的意蕴。到了汉章帝建初元年（公元76年），朝廷为了统一经义，论定谶纬，在洛阳白虎观召开儒学会议，当时的名儒如丁鸿、贾逵、班固等均参加会议。讨论结果由班固编纂成《白虎通义》。

儒家坚持"亲亲""尊尊"的立法原则，维护"礼治"，提倡"德治"，重视"仁治"。儒家思想被封建统治者长期奉为正统思想。从汉代至唐代，河洛地区儒学大家辈出，如贾谊、侯霸、杜子春、孟光、韩愈等，不断推动儒学新发展。

the latter a county magistrate in Luoyang City. As the master of Confucianism, Confucius' arrival in Luoyang shows that his ideology originated from the Duke of Zhou whose ideology was, in turn, formed during his reign in Luoyang. So, we could say Confucianism is deeply rooted in the Heluo region.

Confucian classics flourished in the Heluo region during the Eastern Han Dynasty. As the first emperor of the Eastern Han Dynasty, Liu Xiu was interested in Confucianism and its classics when he was a student at the Imperial College. In the process of establishing his kingdom, Liu Xiu "liked Confucianism and Confucian classics so much so that he used to consult Confucian intellectuals and scholars on what he didn't understand as soon as he visited them." After the founding of his kingdom, Liu Xiu gathered a great number of Confucians and established the Imperial Academy. Emperor Ming, Liu's son, hoped to resolve the crisis of the crown using the systems and the rituals of Confucianism. Furthermore, he, personally, gathered Confucians to discuss the implications of Confucian classics. In the first year of Emperor Zhang's reign (76 AD), the imperial court organized a Confucian conference at the White Tiger Palace in Luoyang to unify the meaning of Confucian classics. Many famous Confucian scholars including Ding Hong, Jia Kui, and Ban Gu attended the conference. The results of the discussion were compiled by Ban Gu into a book titled *The White Tigher Coherent Argumentation of Classics*.

Confucianism adhered to the legislative principle of "affinity" and "respect," advocated "the rule of rituals and virtue" as well as "the rule of benevolence." Hence, for a long time, Confucianism was regarded as orthodoxy. From the Han Dynasty to the Tang Dynasty in the Heluo region, there appeared so many Confucian scholars including Jia Yi, Hou Ba, Du Zichun, Meng Guang, and Han Yu, who all made far-reaching contributions to Confucianism.

二、河洛道教

　　道教创始于洛阳。老子是道家学说的创始人，春秋时在洛阳任周的守藏史，管理图书达30年之久，熟悉夏、商、周以来的各种典章制度。洛阳是当时社会矛盾最集中的地区，老子耳闻目睹了东周王城发生的"王子朝之乱"等重大事件，对争权夺利的内幕、统治者的腐败有着深切的体察与感悟，并出于对人生的无奈和失望，他在暮年辞去官职，骑青牛而去。据说老子西行至函谷关，被关令尹喜发现。老子将自己对宇宙万物的观察了解，对客观事物的认识，对人生的见解，写成《道德经》五千言留给尹喜，之后倒骑青牛飘然而去，从此不知所终。

　　《道德经》是老子在河洛地域创作的重要文献，被后世道教奉为经典，老子被视为道家宗师，被奉为道教的三位尊神之一的道德天尊。老子认为，"道"是天地万物生成的动力之源，"道生一、一生二、二生三、三生万物""人法地，地法天，天法道，道法自然""天下万物生于有，有生于无"。概括而言，《道德经》在哲学上，主张"道"是天地万物之始之母，阴阳对立与统一是万物的本质体现，物极必反是万物演化的规律；伦理上，主张纯朴、无私、清静、谦让、贵柔、守弱、淡泊等因循自然的德性；政治上，主张对内无为而治，不生事扰民，对外和平共处，反对战争与暴力。

　　老子及庄子之学在发展过程中先形成黄老之学，后与神仙学的方士仙道结合形成黄老道，遂演化为道教。黄老道在洛阳地区广泛流传，汉明帝和汉章帝时，朝廷上下以崇信黄老为风气。汉桓帝时，独尊"黄老道"，在洛阳濯龙宫中，专祭黄帝、老子。太平道是黄老道在河洛地区发展的一个支脉，在汉灵帝时期，张角在研究了《太平清领书》后，创立太平道，洛阳城中许多市民、官吏，甚至皇宫中的宦官，都是太平道的信徒。黄老道另一个支脉的发展虽不在河洛地区，但其创始人张道陵

II. Taoism in the Heluo Region

Taoism originated in Luoyang. As the founder of Taoism, Lao Tzu was the curator of the national library of the Zhou Dynasty in Luoyang for about thirty years and was well acquainted with all sorts of decrees and regulations about the Xia Dynasty (2070 BC-1600 BC), Shang Dynasty (1600 BC-1046 BC), and Zhou Dynasty(1046 BC-256 BC). At that time, Luoyang was full of crises and conflicts. Lao Tzu had heard and saw major events that happened in Luoyang City including the Succession Battle of Emperor Ji Zhao. The power struggles and the corruption made him feel helpless and disappointed toward life thereby leading to his resignation from office in his twilight year and starting a new journey toward the west with a black ox. According to the historical records, Lao Tzu met the official Yin Xi at Hangu Guan Pass and left him with a classic of *Tao Te Ching*— a record of his thoughts on the universe, all things including the life of human beings. He continued his journey with the black ox and no one heard of him thereafter.

Tao Te Ching was written in the Heluo region by Lao Tzu. This book has been praised as a classic, and Lao Tzu has thus been called the master of Taoism, and has been worshipped as Taote Prime, one of the three deities of Taoism. Lao Tzu suggests that Taoism is the cradle of the universe of all things, and "Tao produces one (universe), one produces two (yin and yang), two produce three (of heaven, earth, and man), and three gives rise to the universe of all things... Men are abstracted from the earth, the earth from the heaven, the heaven from Tao, and Tao from nature ...The universe of all things is born of being or nothingness." In a word, *Tao Te Ching* argues that Tao is the beginning of all things, the essence of all things is both unified and contradictory, and things develop in opposite directions when they become extreme from the philosophical point of view. From the view of ethics, Tao approves a natural virtue of being innocent, selfless, quiet, modest, gentle, indifferent, and a low profile. Tao politically advocates that the emperor should govern people without intervention or disturbance, create a peaceful coexistence relationship with other countries, and fight against war and violence.

The School of Lao Tzu and Chuang Tzu gradually developed into the

与洛阳有密切的关系。他奉老子为教主，创立"五斗米道"（因受治之人出五斗米而得名），此被视为中国道教之始。但张道陵在汉顺帝时潜心参悟、修道之处是在河洛嵩山和北邙山，"周流五岳，精思积感，真降道成，号曰天师"。

道教的成熟应归功于北魏嵩山道士寇谦之的改革。寇谦之隐居嵩山修道30余年，在得到北魏最高统治者的信任后对天师道进行大刀阔斧的改革。他改革道教的简明纲领是：除去三张伪法、租米钱税及男女合气之术；专以礼度为首，而加以服食闭练。新天师道奉太上老君为最高神，以清虚为本旨，更强调通过养生修炼达到长生不老，同时注重符箓，斋戒沐浴，烧炼金丹，皆有科仪。天师道经此改革，具备了较强的宗教力量，对道教的发展起到了里程碑式的作用。寇谦之出道后，大部分时间活动在中岳庙，道教尊中岳庙为"第六小洞天"。

隋唐以降，河洛地区道教兴盛不衰。隋炀帝对道教宠信有加，在洛阳城特置道术坊，让具有道术的人居住。唐高宗在北邙山原老子祠处建上清宫，追加老子"太上玄元皇帝"的最高尊号。嵩山道士潘诞、潘师正、司马承祯等，都是这一时期著名道教人物。宋元时期一些道士如吕洞宾、朗然子等先后在洛阳传道。金代以前，道教出现宗派，河洛地区先后流行的道教有"正一道""太一道""真大道"。后陕西王重阳所创的全真道在河洛兴起后，北七真中有谭长真、刘长生、孙不二在洛阳修真传道，留下云溪观、风仙洞等史迹。

Huang-Lao School before combining, subsequently, with the necromancy of immortal-Taoism to become Huang-Lao Taoism. Eventually, the Taoism came into being. The Huang-Lao Taoism was widely spread in the Luoyang region. At the time of Emperor Ming and Emperor Zhang of the Han Dynasty, it was popular to worship Huang-Lao Taoism all over the country. In the Han Dynasty, Emperor Huan just venerated the Huang-Lao Taoism and only worshiped the Yellow Emperor and Lao Tzu at Zhuolong Palace, Luoyang. Taiping Taoism is a branch of Huang-Lao Taoism in the Heluo region. During the reign of Emperor Ling in the Han Dynasty (168 AD-189 AD), Zhang Jiao studied the *Taiping Scriptures* and founded Taiping Taoism. At that time, many citizens, officials, and court eunuchs believed in Taiping Taoism. The other branch of Huang-Lao Taoism didn't develop in the Heluo region. However, its founder, Zhang Daoling, has a close relationship with Luoyang. Zhang regarded Lao Tzu as the master and set up the "Five-dou-grain Taoism" (one needs to pay a tax of five-dou-grain to join the clique). This was the beginning of Taoism in China. During the reign of Emperor Shun in the Han Dynasty, Zhang went to Songshan Moutain and Northern Mangshan Mountain to seek truth from meditation. According to historical records, "Zhang went to Songshan Mountain and lived in a stone cavern for about nine years. He traveled the Five Mountains of China to seek truth from meditation. Eventually, he became enlightened and he gained praise as Celestial Master."

Taoism gradually matured after Kou qianzhi,'s reform. Kou qianzhi, a Taoist priest of Songshan Mountain in the Northern Wei Dynasty, lived in seclusion for about thirty years. Thereafter, he was authorized, by the then emperor, to carry out the reform of Celestial-Master Taoism. His brief guideline was to "get rid of the thoughts of Three Zhang, exempt the grain taxes and sexual intercourse in Taoism. Taoism is so pure and void that priests must follow the regulations and take medicine to be enlightened" (*The Book of the Wei Dynasty: Shi Lao Zhi*). Lao Tzu was regarded as the supreme god in Neo-Celestial-Master Taoism, whose purpose was pure and void. Neo-Celestial-Master Taoism emphasized living forever by preserving health, drawing signs, abstaining from meat, taking a shower, and refining golden cinnabar. After the reform, the Celestial-Master Taoism owned a stronger religious power that played a landmark role in the development of Taoism. Kou qianzhi spent most of his time in the temple of Songshan Mountain

图3-2　洛阳上清宫
Figure 3-2　Shang Qing Palace in Luoyang

　　河洛著名道教宫观有上清宫、下清宫、吕祖庙、中岳庙等。上清宫坐落在洛阳市老城西北约4公里的邙山之巅翠云峰上，相传是道教始祖李耳炼丹的地方。上清宫门外有石狮石马，内有吴道子所作壁画《吴圣图》和《老子化胡经》，十分辉煌、壮观。唐诗人杜甫于天宝八年（749年）到此，写出《冬日洛城北谒玄元皇帝庙》诗文，传下"山河扶绣户，日月近雕梁"的名句，给后人描绘了当时洛阳的锦绣河山和壮观皇城。下清宫位于上清宫东南的邙岭半坡处，传说是老子上翠云峰炼丹时的拴牛之地。这里也是洛阳八景中"邙山晚眺"的观景点。

and that explains why the temple is also known as the Sixth Cave of Taoism.

Taoism in the Heluo region has thrived since the Sui and Tang dynasties. Emperor Yang of the Sui Dynasty preferred Taoism, so he accommodated Taoist priests who held workshops in Luoyang City. During the Tang Dynasty, Emperor Gao Zong commanded people to build a Shang Qing Palace in the old site of the ancestral temple of Lao Tzu at the northern Mangshan Mountain and gave Lao Tzu the supreme title "Emperor Taishang Xuanyuan." At that time, there were so many famous Taoist priests including Pan Dan, Pan Shizheng, and Sima Chengzhen. In the Song and Yuan dynasties, Lv Dongbin and Lang Ranzi propagated Taoism in Luoyang. Before the Jin Dynasty, there were some branches of Taoism and in the Heluo region, Zhengyi Taoism, Taiyi Taoism, and Zhenda Taoism prevailed. Later, Wang Chongyang founded Quanzhen Taoism in the Heluo region. Besides, Tan Changzhen, Liu Changsheng, and Sun Buer preached Taoism in Luoyang, and they built historic temples including the Cloud and Stream Temple as well as the Wind God Temple.

There are many famous Taoist temples in the Heluo region. For example, Shang Qing Palace, Xia Qing Palace, Lvzu Temple, Songshan Mountain Taoist Temple. Shang Qing Palace is located at the top of Mangshan Mountain, which is about four kilometers away from the northwest of Old City District, Luoyang. It is believed that it was at this place that Lao Tzu refined the cinnabar. There are stone carvings of lions and horses outside Shang Qing Palace. In the inner walls, Wu Daozi, the famous painter drew wonderful pictures including *Wu Sheng's Picture* and the *Figure of Lao Tzu Fetching Scriptures*. In the eighth year of Tianbao (749 AD), Du Fu, the famous poet, arrived there and wrote the poem *Visiting Xuanyuan Temple, Luoyang, on a Winter Day*. In the poem, he wrote "mountains and rivers surround embroidered households, and the sun and the moon shine on their roofs", describing the beautiful, splendid, and magnificent imperial Luoyang City. Xia Qing Palace, known as the Black Ox Temple, is situated southeast of Shang Qing Palace. It is the place where Lao Tzu set his black ox whenever he went to Yuncui Mountain to do alchemy. At the same time, this place is referred to as "the best view overlooking Mangshan Mountain at dusk," and it is one of the greatest among the best eight great points in Luoyang City.

三、河洛佛教

佛教首传于洛阳。佛教起源于公元前6—5世纪的古印度,传入中国的正式记载,是在东汉明帝时期。《弘明集》卷一记载:昔孝明皇帝梦见神人,身有日光,飞在殿前,欣然悦之。明日,博问群臣:"此为何神?"有通人傅毅曰:"臣闻天竺有得道者,号之曰佛,飞行虚空,身有日光,殆将其神也。"于是,汉明帝遣蔡愔等人出使天竺,求取佛经佛法。永平十年(67年),使臣返回洛阳,带回天竺高僧摄摩腾和竺法兰。同时,用白马驮回《四十二章经》。汉明帝礼重二僧,让他们住在鸿胪寺传教译经。次年,敕令在西雍门外三里御道北修造僧院,因白马驮经来,遂取名白马寺。白马寺是佛教传入中国后的第一座官办寺院,也是古印度佛教在中华大地上的第一座菩提道场,因此被尊称为中国佛教的"祖庭"和"释源",对佛教在中国的传播和发展,对促进中外思想文化交流和发展各国人民的友谊,起了重要的作用。

图3-3　洛阳白马寺
Figure 3-3　White Horse Temple

III. Buddhism in the Heluo Region

First, Buddhism came to Luoyang. Buddhism originated in ancient India from the sixth century to the fifth century BC, and according to historical records, it was introduced into China during the reign of Emperor Ming of the Eastern Han Dynasty. The first volume of *The Book of the Later Han Dynasty* maintains that Emperor Ming, Liu Zhuang, was delighted with his dream about a shining golden saint flying in front of the imperial palace one day in the eighth year of Yong Ping's reign (65 AD). The next day, Emperor Ming summoned his ministers for an explanation. Fu Yi, a learned minister replied, "there is a western god called Buddha in India who can fly in the sky with a divine light." After that, Emperor Ming sent Envoy Cai Yin and others to fetch the Buddhist Sutras from India. In the tenth year of Yong Ping (67 AD), the ambassadors returned to Luoyang with *The Sutra in Forty-two Sections*. At the same time, the monks Kasyapamatanga (She Moteng) and Dharmaraksa (Zhu Falan) also arrived in Luoyang. Emperor Ming greeted the two monks with warm and gracious hospitality and arranged that they preach and translate the sutras at David Bunch Temple. In the next year, he ordered to build a Buddhist temple at the north of the national highway located three li away from Xiyongmen Gate, Luoyang. This Buddhist temple was later called the White Horse Temple because *The Sutra in Forty-two Sections* was carried by a white horse. The White Horse Temple was the first official temple since Buddhism was first preached in China. Therefore, it is reserved as the Ancestral Hall and Origin of Buddhism in China. It has made great contributions to the spread and development of Buddhism in China, the promotion of cultural exchanges and friendship between China and other countries.

During the Wei and Jin dynasties, many Buddhists in the Western Regions went to the Heluo region to preach Buddhism and its sutras, so the translation of the sutras continued to flourish in Luoyang. In the second year of the reign of Jia Ping (250 AD), Tanke Jialuo, an Indian, arrived in Luoyang and translated the *Volume of Monk*. He gathered the monks in Luoyang and created relevant rites and systems that monks must respect. In addition, he established the Chinese Ritsu in Luoyang. After that, Tanke Jialuo was called the ancestor of Ritsu. In

魏晋时期，西域佛教徒游化河洛地区仍络绎不绝，译经事业在洛阳继续开展。嘉平二年（250年），中天竺僧昙柯迦罗来到洛阳，译出《僧祇戒心》一卷。他又广集在洛阳的梵僧，商议订立出家为僧的仪式及应遵守的制度，在洛阳建立了中国律宗的基础。因此，后世人称昙柯迦罗为律宗的始祖。甘露五年（公元260年），洛阳人朱士行在白马寺受戒出家，成为中国的第一个正式僧人，并西行取经，在今新疆和田取得了《大品般若》，于晋武帝太康三年（公元282年）送回洛阳，成为内地往西域求法的第一个僧人。这时佛教也开始由中原地区向江南发展。

北魏时期洛阳是佛教世界的国际名都。当时僧尼社会地位颇高，许多皇后嫔妃以出家为尼为荣，孝文帝皇后冯氏居瑶光寺为尼以终。宣武帝皇后高氏，在延昌三年（514年）三月，也到瑶光寺出家为尼。北魏时期洛阳佛寺达1367所，侈丽瑰奇，冠于宇内。其中最为著名的是永宁寺。永宁寺是北魏孝明帝时建造，金碧辉煌，其中木制九层浮屠，高90丈，刹上有宝瓶，宝瓶下有承露金盘三十重，周匝皆垂金铎，仅门扉装有5400枚金钉，并有金环铺首。印度僧人菩提达摩来到洛阳时，见永宁寺"金盘炫目，光照云表；宝铎含风，响出天外。歌咏赞叹，实是神功，自云：'历涉诸国，靡不周遍，而此寺精丽，阎浮所无也，极佛境界，亦未有此'"。永宁寺塔在北魏永熙三年（534年）被雷电击中焚毁。1979年在永宁寺遗址发掘过程中，出土了一批精美的北魏泥塑像，其面部表情、发髻、服饰、籍巾等形态各异，造型精致。这些佛教造像艺术价值极高，而且为研究魏晋南北朝时期的佛教与民族关系，提供了实物资料。

少林寺，创建于北魏太和二十年（496年），因为此寺建于少室山麓的丛林茂密之处，故名"少林"。这里群山环拱，满目青翠，古寺峥嵘，高塔林立，别有洞天。据文献记载，北魏太和十九年（495年）印度高僧跋陀自西域跋涉来洛阳，他性爱幽栖，常到嵩山，又受孝文帝

the fifth year of the reign of Ganlu (260 AD), Zhu Shixing, the first formal monk in the historical records, accepted the Buddhist ordination and became a monk in the White Horse Temple. Then, he went to the west to consult the Buddhist sutras. Eventually, he fetched the *Da Pin Prajna* from the Hetian region in Xinjiang Province and returned to Luoyang in the third year of the reign of Taikang in the Jin Dynasty (282 AD). Zhu became the first inlander who went to the West Regions to learn the Buddhist sutras. At that time, Buddhism started to transmit from central China to southern China.

Luoyang is the international capital of Buddhism in the Northern Wei Dynasty. At that time, monks and nuns enjoyed a high social status so many empresses and concubines were proud of being nuns. For example, Feng, Emperor Xiaowen's empress, became a nun in the Yaoguang Temple; Gao, Emperor Xuanwu's empress, also chose to be a nun in the March of the third year of Yanchang (514 AD). Up until the Northern Wei Dynasty, there were 1,367 Buddhist temples in the Luoyang region most of which were magnificent and wonderful with outstanding facades. The most famous was Yongning Temple and it was founded during the reign of Emperor Xiaoming in the Northern Wei Dynasty. Resplendent with golden decorations, Yongning Temple boasted a facade with a wooden nine-layer stupa that was 90 *zhangs* tall. Inside the temple, there was a treasure bottle above Chenglu golden plates. Around the 30 plates, there were hangings of golden *duos* (a kind of ancient Chinese musical instrument). On the door, there were over 5,400 golden nails and numerous golden rings. The Indian monk Bodhidharma visited Yongming Temple in Luoyang, and looking at the golden plates shining with a dazzling light and the golden *duo* tinkling in the gentle breeze, said with admiration, "I have visited many temples all around the world, and I've never seen one so splendid and wonderful. There are no other temples like this one." Yongning Temple was ruined by thunder and lightning in the third year of Yongxi (534 AD) in the Northern Wei Dynasty. In 1979, during the excavations of the ruins of Yongning Temple, a batch of delicate clay figures were discovered. These Buddhist figures looked exquisite with different countenances, hair buns, dresses, and scarfs.

Built in the twentieth year of Taihe in the Northern Wei Dynasty (496 AD), Shaolin Temple was named after its location at the foot of Shaoshishan

图3-4　洛阳龙门
Figure 3-4　Longmen Grottoes

尊崇，下诏于少室山阴，筑少林寺而居之。北魏孝昌三年（527年），菩提达摩东渡，自江南北上洛阳，到少林寺修禅。迄今少林寺僧徒还盛传达摩"一苇渡江"的故事。达摩居少林寺9年，他广集弟子，传授禅宗。禅宗的基调是以心性论为基点，倡导即心是佛、见性成佛，主张寂坐修心，用"壁观"的办法，面壁静坐，使"心如壁立，不偏不倚"，从而摆脱烦恼、追求生命自觉。达摩被尊为中国佛教禅宗初祖，少林禅寺也成为禅宗的"祖庭"。少林寺历经千余年的历史沧桑，至今仍规模宏大，雄风犹存，是驰名海内外的名胜风景。

Mountain. It was surrounded by mountains with green trees and grass and the high towers that stood in the outstanding ancient temple adding glory to a beautiful scenery. According to historical records, Bhatta, an eminent Indian monk, arrived in Luoyang from the Western Regions in the nineteenth year of Taihe in the Northern Wei Dynasty (495 AD). He used to go to Songshan Mountain to find a sequestered place. Emperor Xiaowen respected Bhatta and ordered him to build Shaolin Temple north of Shaoshishan Mountain. In the third year of Xiaochang in the Northern Wei Dynasty (527 AD), Bodhidharma went from the south of China to Luoyang, and he also studied Zen Buddhism in Shaolin Temple. Hence, the story of Bodhidharma Crossing the River with A Reed is also popular nowadays. Bodhidharma lived in Shaolin Temple for about nine years and he had many disciples to transmit the Zen. As the foundation of Zen Buddhism, the theory of mind-nature emphasizes the mind as the seat of

北魏至唐代，佛教凿窟雕像也成为风气。河洛地区有名的佛教石窟有龙门石窟、巩义石窟、水泉石窟、西沃石窟等。龙门石窟位于洛阳南12.5公里的伊河两岸的龙门山和香山，开凿于北魏孝文帝年间，之后历经东魏、西魏、北齐、隋、唐、五代、宋等朝代连续大规模营造达400余年之久，今存有窟龛2345个，造像10万余尊，碑刻题记2800余品。卢舍那大佛，位于龙门石窟的奉先寺，据碑文记载为"大唐高宗天皇大帝之所建也，皇后助脂粉钱二万贯"。佛高17.14米，头部高4米，耳长1.9米，为龙门石窟最大之造像。佛像面容丰满秀丽，二目宁静慈祥，姿态端庄肃穆，衣纹简洁流畅，具有形神兼备的效果。两侧侍立弟子迦叶严谨含蓄，阿难温顺虔诚，菩萨头戴宝冠，身着璎珞，衣带飘洒，端庄矜持。天王蹙眉怒目，气势威武；力士则筋肌突暴，猛壮刚健。不同人物的性格刻画得惟妙惟肖、多姿多彩，充分显示了盛唐雕塑艺术的高度成就。2000年，龙门石窟被联合国教科文组织评价为"中国石刻艺术的最高峰"，列入世界文化遗产。

河洛地区也出现了中国佛教史上有影响的高僧。慧可，少通老庄、易学，满腹经纶，世传其曾"立雪断臂"向达摩求法，表示自己求道的恳切和决心。支遁，曾在洛阳白马寺纵谈《庄子·逍遥篇》，标揭新理，名噪一时，成为魏晋玄学与佛教般若学交融的重要人物。道安，东晋穆帝升平四年（360年）为避难来到洛阳嵩县陆浑，在此历经磨难，曾以木为食。他制定了僧规、经录，统一了出家人的姓氏，总结了佛经汉译的经验，提出了"五失本，三不易"的翻译原则。玄奘，洛阳偃师缑氏人，他完成艰苦卓绝的西行求法壮举，往返行程五万里，历56国，从印度带回大小乘三藏经典520册、657部，以及佛像、舍利等，为佛教原典文献的研究与传播做出巨大贡献。此外，洛阳还聚集了许多番僧，如菩提流志、实叉难陀、提云般若、金刚智、不空、善无畏、弥陀山等。他们多是由朝廷重礼聘请而到洛阳的，同时还带来了重要的梵文佛经，这也使洛阳成为重要的译经道场。

Buddhism and sitting silently toward the wall as a way to cultivate the mind. To pursue the notion of awakening to life, Zen ensured Buddhists stayed away from any irritation to become upright and innocent. Bodhidharma is praised as the primary ancestor of Chinese Zen Buddhism, and Shaolin Temple is also called the Ancestral Hall of Buddhism. After several thousand years, Shaolin Temple, with its grand scale and outstanding structures, is still a famous scenic spot at home and abroad.

The sculpture of Buddhist statues became very popular from the Northern Wei Dynasty to the Tang Dynasty. The famous Buddhist grottoes in the Heluo region include Longmen Grottoes, Gongxian County Grottoes, Shuiquan Grottoes, and Xiwo Grottoes. Longmen Grottoes are located 12.5 kilometers south of Luoyang City. They sit face to face on both sides of the Yi River that runs in between the two opposite hills—Longmen Hill and Fragrant Hill. It was built in the reign of Emperor Xiaowen. After that, it continued to be enlarged during the Eastern Wei, Western Wei, Northern Qi, Sui, Tang, Five Dynasties, Song and other dynasties for over 400 years. Nowadays, Longmen grottoes consist of over 2,345 niches, 100,000 statues and 2,800 inscriptions and steles. Vairocana Buddha is located in the Fengxian Si (the Ancestor Worshiping Cave) of the Longmen Grottoes on which are inscribed the words: " It was built by Emperor Gao Zong of the Tang Dynasty, and the Empress paid 20,000 Guan of money for it." Vairocana Buddha, with its 17.4-meter height, 4-meter-tall head, and 1.9-meter-long ears, is the biggest statue of the Longmen Grottoes. With kind eyes, a plump and beautiful countenance, the Buddha stands dignifiedly and solemnified, covered with simple and fluent clothing. On both sides of Buddha stand Kasyapa and Ananda, who wear crowns, jewelry, and silk tassels. The former is a strict and reserved disciple; the latter is docile and devout. Both of them are dignified and reserved. Devatas frowns with staring eyes and with robust muscles while Mahabalavan is strong and energetic. Different chapters have unique and vivid images that show the greatest achievements of the sculptural art of the Tang Dynasty. In 2000, the Longmen Grottoes were evaluated by the United Nations Educational, Scientific and Cultural Organization as "the high peak of Chinese stone carving" and was successfully inscribed upon the UNESCO World Heritage List.

图3-5 龙门卢舍那大佛
Figure 3-5 Sculpture of Vairochana Buddha in Longmen Grottoes

自宋代之后,随着国家政治中心和经济重心的南移,佛教在河洛地区逐渐衰落了,大批的寺院也在兵荒马乱中毁于战火,佛教徒大批南迁,河洛地区的佛教由盛而衰。

Heluo region was the cradle of eminent monks who had a significant impact on Chinese Buddhism. Hui Ke, a learned monk, had a good knowledge of Lao Tzu and Chuang Tzu Yiology. According to the historical records, Hui Ke pursued the truth from Dharma and his story Dying the Snow with Blood showed his earnestness and determination for Buddhist truth. As an important component of the Metaphysics of the Wei and Jin dynasties and Buddhist Prajna, Zhi Dun talked eloquently about *The Records of Chuang Tzu* in the White Horse Temple as a way of revealing the new rules that were popular at that time. In the fourth year of Shengping in the Eastern Jin Dynasty, Dao An came to Luhun Town in Song County, Luoyang. He lived a hard life there at one point having to feed on wood. However, he drew up regulations and sutras about monks and unified the surnames of Buddhists. Furthermore, he summarized the experience of translating Buddhist sutras into Chinese and put forward the translation principle of Five Losts and Three Unchanged Rules. The monk Xuan Zang was a native Gou from Yanshi County in Luoyang City. He undertook an arduous 50,000-kilometer journey during which he crossed 56 countries to the Western Regions in the pursuit of Dharma. He returned from India to Luoyang with 520 Mahayana classics, 657 Hinayana sutras, several Buddhas, and Buddhist relics that significantly contributed to the study and dissemination of the original Buddhist version. In addition, because they were invited by the imperial court with a high retainer fee, many foreign monks including Bodhiruci, Siksananda, Devaprajna, Vajrabodhi, Amoghavajra, Subhakara-simha, and Amitabha gathered in Luoyang. At the same time, many precious Sanskrit Buddhist scriptures were carried to Luoyang, which transformed Luoyang into an influential venue for translation.

Since the Song Dynasty, the political and economic center gradually transferred to the south of China. During the war, a large number of temples were destroyed and the Buddhists left for the south of China. Therefore, Buddhism in the Heluo region went from prosperity to decline.

四、河洛玄学

　　玄学兴盛于洛阳。玄学是魏晋时期兴起的一种崇尚老庄的哲学思潮。它的产生、形成、发展和衰落主要是在魏晋时期，因此人们又称其为魏晋玄学。玄学的命名来源于《老子》的"玄之又玄，众妙之门"，"玄"就是深远的意思。玄学崇尚老庄，把《老子》《庄子》《周易》称之为"三玄"。

　　玄学产生和发展的过程大体经历了正始玄学、竹林玄学、西晋玄学三个不同的阶段，河洛地区是其发展、演变之地。原因在于这一时期的洛阳帝都时局动荡，从曹氏篡汉到司马氏篡魏，权力斗争异常激烈，统治者一方面依靠门阀世族来维护政权，另一方面，又残酷地排斥、诛杀异己，迥然不同于先前稳定的大一统的汉王朝统治。政治的纷争，隐藏着难以预料的风险；乱世险恶，引发了深广的忧思。世态炎凉，朝不保夕，社会的黑暗与生命意识的觉醒，恰恰给自先秦以来的又一次思想大解放创造了条件。特别是身处帝都权力舞台的士大夫为了避开政治迫害的罗网，往往避世隐逸，清淡无为，甚至佯狂放荡，玩世不恭，倾心于"玄虚淡泊，与道逍遥"，而这构成了以河洛地区为中心的玄学兴起的时代与文化背景。

　　正始玄学的代表人物，是曹魏正始年间的何晏和王弼。何晏是曹操养子，生性豁达，无拘无束，好老庄之言，倡导玄学。他宣称"天地万物以无为本"，主张君主无为而治。王弼倡论"无"是宇宙万物的本体，认为"天下之物，皆以有为生。有之所始，以无为本。将欲全有，必反于无也"。他既重视作为"本"的"无"与作为"末"的"有"之间的关系，更从认识论的高度提出"举本统末""崇本息末"的思想主张。何晏、王弼用老庄玄虚的道理讲《周易》，即援老子的思想、观点入儒学，完全改变了汉儒以象数之学讲《周易》的性质，从根本上冲破

IV. Metaphysics in the Heluo Region

Metaphysics, a philosophy following the ideas of Lao Tzu and Chuang Tzu, prospered in Luoyang during the Wei and Jin dynasties. It is during these two dynasties that Metaphysics originated, formed, developed, and declined. Therefore, Metaphysics is also called the Wei and Jin dynasties' Metaphysics. Metaphysics was named by Lao Tzu whose classic *Tao Te Ching* reads, "Metaphysics is the one and only way to all mysteries." Metaphysics refers to profound and abstract things. By worshipping Lao Tzu and Chuang Tzu, Metaphysics regarded *Tao Te Ching*, *Chuang Tzu*, and *The Book of Changes* as the "Three Books of Metaphysics."

Generally, there were three developmental stages of Metaphysics: Metaphysics in the period of Zhengshi, Bamboo Grove Metaphysics, and the Western Jin Dynasty Metaphysics. They all developed and evolved in the Heluo region. At that time, the political situation was a mess and power struggles were extremely fierce in Luoyang. For instance, Cao usurped the Han Dynasty while Sima overturned the Wei Dynasty. On the one hand, the current ruler wanted to maintain his regime by consolidating power in the hands of one family through the system of one family power and influence, and on the other hand, he excluded and killed his dissidents, action that was in complete contrast to the grand unification of the Han Dynasty. The political struggles led to unpredictable risks and the troubled times made people feel uneasy and worried. The gloomy prospect of society and the awakening of consciousness about life created a condition that once again, ever since the pre-Qin period, liberated people's thinking. In order to hide the political persecutions, some scholar-officials, especially those in the capital, Luoyang, chose to retire from the world, lived in seclusion, or pretended to be mad. Due to their affection for Metaphysics, most of them refused to seek fame and wealth. That explains why Metaphysics prospered in the Luoyang region.

He Yan and Wang Bi typically represent the concept of Metaphysics in the Zhengshi period during the Three Kingdoms Period (220 AD-280 AD). As the foster son of General Cao Cao, He Yan was open-minded and unrestrained. He had profound admiration of the thoughts of Lao Tzu and Chuang Tzu and

图3-6 老子骑青牛出关
Figure 3-6　A Stone Sculpture of Lao Tzu

advocated for Metaphysics claiming that "nothingness is the essence of the universe." He proposed that the emperor should govern the state by doing nothing and just follow nature. Wang Bi argued that "nothingness" is the *substance* of all things in the universe, and "all things in the universe survive by being while being is the initial point of nothingness. Things evolve in the opposite direction if they go the extreme way." He attached great importance to the relations between the beginning of "nothingness" and the ending of "being" on the one hand, and, from an epistemology viewpoint, put forward the philosophy of "worshiping the beginning and paying less attention to the ending" on the other hand. He Yan and Wang Bi preached *The Book of Changes* through the Metaphysics of Lao Tzu and Chuang Tzu thereby combining Taoism with Confucianism. This point overturned the traditional way of interpreting this book by Confucians in the Han Dynasty and broke the essence of Confucianism in the Eastern and Western dynasties.

Ji Kang and Ruan Ji are famous representatives of the Bamboo Grove Metaphysics. The former put forward the fundamental notion of "getting over the Confucian ethical code but letting nature at ease" and proposed that everyone is independent and should follow nature. He fought against the bondage of Confucianism and emphasized that "people should focus on the right path and engage in behaviors that follow Tao." Furthermore, he pointed out the conflicts between the theory of "sound without a dirge" and "musical education," in some sense, and showed his pursuit of the ideal personality through good health maintenance. Ruan Ji worked in Luoyang for a long time. He looked down upon the feudal ethical code and "the people who admire rituals." Later, to survive terrible political struggles, he indulged in drinking rather than praising or dissing anyone else. Advocating that "the universe is born in nature and all things are born in the universe," he claimed that "nature" and the feudal system should be integrated, and everyone should follow the rule whereby "no one bullies their subordinates and no one goes against their superiors." Represented by Ruan Ji and Ji Kang, the Bamboo Grove Metaphysics and the art of their behaviors created "Wei-Jin style" and "unconventional and unrestrained behavior of talented scholars."

Pei Wei, Xiang Xiu, and Guo Xiang are the three representatives of

了两汉儒学的思想本源。

竹林玄学的代表人物是嵇康和阮籍。嵇康提出"越名教而任自然"的玄学观点，主张人应自然而为，强调个体人格的独立性，反对儒教的束缚。"心无措乎是非，而行不违乎道"。他论述了"声无哀乐"论与"乐教"之冲突，并通过论养生，寄托了对理想人格的追求。阮籍，长期在洛阳任职，蔑视礼教，常以"白眼"看待"礼俗之士"；后期则变为"口不臧否人物"，常"纵酒昏酣，遗落世事"，在当时复杂的政治斗争中保全自己。他认为"天地生于自然，万物生于天地"，主张把"自然"和封建等级制度相结合，做到"在上而不凌乎下，处卑而不犯乎贵"。以阮籍、嵇康为代表的"竹林玄学"及其行为艺术，造就了"魏晋风度""名士风流"。

西晋玄学的代表人物是裴頠、向秀和郭象。裴頠，西晋后期在洛阳当官，撰写《崇有论》，认为"名教"本身就是本体，所以人们应该"崇有"而不是"贵无"。向秀，代表作为《庄子注》，主张自然与明教统一，合儒道为一，认为万物自生自化，所以各任其性，即是"逍遥"。郭象，认为无不能生有，天地万物都是自己生出来的，独立的自身变化，并没有一个外界的力量来推动它们，这即是"独化"。他还提出"万物独化于玄冥之境"，"万物各有定分"，"万物各适其性"。郭象以"独化"论为核心，构建了一个完整、庞大的玄学思辨体系，代表了魏晋玄学发展的最高成就。

玄学思潮的兴起，探讨、反思人自身的价值和文化价值，对两汉以来以外在的功业、节操、学问为特征的价值观念发生了怀疑和动摇，而转向对自己生命、命运、生活、意义的重新发现、思索与追求。所以，玄学思潮实质上标志着一种人的觉醒。何、王、阮、嵇、向、郭等大师，在洛阳兴起、发展了玄学，这是洛阳对华夏人文文化的又一贡献。

Metaphysics in the Western Jin Dynasty (266 AD-316 AD). Pei Wei, the author of *All Things Come From Being*, took office at Luoyang in the late Western Jin Dynasty. He argued that "the Confucian ethical code" is the being, so people should worship "being" rather than "nothingness." Xiang Xiu is the author of *Annotation on Chuang Tzu*. He proposed that nature, Zoroastrianism, and Confucianism should be integrated. Besides, all things in the universe are born and they grow based on their own rules that can be considered free and unfettered. Guo Xiang proposed that "nothingness" is not the initial point of "being," and all things in the universe are independently born by themselves. This concept, according to him, is called "individualization" given that there is no external power that creates things. Also, he put forward the view that "everything is born out of the space of Metaphysics" and "all things have their own rules and follow their own essences." Building on the theory of "individualization" as the core of his thought, Guo Xiang founded a complete and grand system of Metaphysics, which represents the highest accomplishment of the Wei and Jin dynasties.

The rise of Metaphysics was conductive to exploring and reflecting one's own value and cultural value. Its appearance resulted in value conflicts about merit, integrity and learning, after that, people began to recover, rethink and pursue the meaning of their own beings, destiny, and lives since the Eastern and Western Han Dynasty (202 BC-220 AD). In a word, Metaphysics is the signal of the awakening of people. Many masters such as He Yan, Wang Bi, Ji Kang, Ruan Ji, Pei Wei, Xiang Xiu and Guo Xiang developed Metaphysics in the Luoyang region, which made a great contribution to the Huaxia culture.

五、河洛理学

理学光大于洛阳

北宋时期，以程颢、程颐为代表的新儒学——理学，面对佛老思想的挑战，以儒家伦理为本位，批判地吸取佛、道精致的思辨哲学，创建了"洛学"或曰"伊洛理学"。前人提到这一时期，常说"五星聚奎，伊洛钟秀"。朱熹《伊洛渊源录》认为，道学起于周敦颐、程颢、程颐、邵雍、张载等"五星"学者。

邵雍，30多岁时游览洛阳，结识了司马光、富弼等人。司马光出资为其在洛河南岸购置房舍田园，邵雍遂落籍于此，名其园宅为"安乐窝"，自号为安乐先生。邵雍对河图洛书的研究卓有成就。他通过对河图洛书以及伏羲八卦、《六十四卦图象》等的研究，推演出《先天图》，并由此创立了一种以先天图象来解释世界生成演变、推算古往今来治乱兴衰和事物变化的"先天象数学"。他以"心为太极"，主张"万物皆生于心"。邵雍研究"先天之学"，将原来仅仅是社会兴衰、历史变迁、道德教化的人文关怀，最终都与自在宇宙的永恒轮回、先天世界的终极存在联系在一起，从而获得了形而上的终极意义，为北宋的儒学确立了一种立足于儒家人文价值的终极信仰。南宋朱熹对其甚为推崇，列之于"北宋五子"之中。

在"北宋五子"中，程颢、程颐兄弟是最重要的人物。二程一生从事于"穷理、识仁、明道"工作，创立了精致、完整而具有思辨性的理学体系。二程理学强调"理"或"天理"。他们认为"理"是自然界遵循的普遍原则，是永恒不变的。它"不为尧存，不为桀亡"。任何人和事物都不能违背"天理"这个最高准则，而"君道""臣道""父道""子道"等都是天理的表现。二程学说以人伦道德即以仁、义、礼、智、信的社会道德法则为天理观的价值指向。他们还提出了"格物

V. Neo-Confucianism in the Heluo Region

Neo-Confucianism flourished in Luoyang

In the Northern Song Dynasty (960 AD-1125 AD), represented by Cheng Hao and Cheng Yi, Neo-Confucianism faced challenges from the thoughts of Buddhism and Taoism. Based on Confucian ethics, the two Cheng brothers critically absorbed the refined speculative philosophy of Buddhism and Taoism and established "Heluo Study," also known as "Neo-Confucianism in the Yiluo region." Whenever people talk about this period, they often say, " It was the period that Five Stars got together and the culture in the Yiluo region flourished. According to Zhu Xi's *The History of Yiluo*, the "Five Stars" scholars who established Taoism included Zhou Dunyi, Cheng Hao, Cheng Yi, Shao Yong, and Zhang Zai.

In his thirties, Shao Yong became acquainted with Sima Guang and Fu Bi when he traveled to Luoyang. With the help of sponsor Sima Guang, Shao Yong obtained lands and houses at the southern shore of the Luohe River and settled in Luoyang City. He called his house the "cozy nest" and himself "Mr. Happiness." He made outstanding achievements in the study of Hetu and Luoshu. Having learned Hetu and Luoshu, the Eight Trigrams of Fuxi, and the *Sixty-four Hexagram Images*, Shao Yong found *the Priori Images* and created a kind of "priori astronomical mathematics," which is used to explain the becoming of the universe, the rise and fall in history, and changeable things by priori astronomical images. Shao Yong regarded the mind as Tai Chi, and argued that " the universe of all things originates from the mind." Shao Yong's "study of priori" connected. what is otherwise just humanistic thinking about social upheavals, historical changes and moral education with the eternal reincarnation of the universe and the ultimate existence of a priori world, and thus acquired the ultimate meaning of metaphysics and established a kind of ultimate belief based on the Confucian humanistic value in the Northern Song Dynasty. In the Southern Song Dynasty, Zhu Xi highly recommended Shao's thought and listed him as one of the five persons who made great contribution to Confucianism of the Northern Song Dynasty.

Cheng Yi and Cheng Hao are brothers and they played important roles in

图3-7　程颢　程颐　刘龙/摄
Figure 3-7　The Cheng brothers　Photo by Liu Long

致知"和"正心诚意"的道德修养方法。二程理学后经南宋朱熹的进一步完善,成为宋、元、明、清800多年间封建社会的思想统治基础。程颢和程颐被后世帝王尊称为"夫子"。

二程一生以聚徒讲学为己任,伊洛河流域留下了他们的足迹。二程兄弟在性格、生活态度及为学功夫方面均表现出很大的差异。程颢性

the development of Neo-Confucianism of the Song Dynasty. The two Cheng brothers devoted all their lives to "find out the truth, understand benevolence, and clarify Tao," and eventually established a refined, complete, and speculative system of Neo-Confucianism. They believed in "principle" or " the heavenly principle," which is regarded as a common and eternal principle that exists in nature. This principle will "never be changed by anyone" and no one and nothing can violate this supreme principle of "the heavenly principle." Besides, the heavenly principle is embodied by the relationship between the monarch and his servants, father and his son. According to ethics and morality, the two brothers consider social ethics as the guidance of the heavenly principle, namely, the social ethics of benevolence, righteousness, courtesy, wisdom, and trust. In addition, two ways of cultivating one's morality such as "attain knowledge through studying the essence of things" and "control heart and mind to maintain sincerity" were put forward by the two brothers. The two Cheng brothers' Neo-Confucianism was further perfected by Zhu Xi in the Southern Song dynasty and it became the ideological foundation of the feudal society in the dynasties of Northern Song, Southern Song, Yuan, Ming, and Qing over eight hundred years. Cheng Hao and Cheng Yi were praised as "Master" by later emperors.

By giving lectures to their disciples, the two Cheng Brothers left their footprints in the region of the Yihe River and Luoyang River in their whole lives. They showed a great difference in many aspects including character, attitude toward life, and capability. Cheng Hao was gentle, funny, and gave his students a feeling of "spring breeze." Cheng Yi, on the contrary, was strict and careful. He paid attention to the dignity of the teacher and expressed a feeling of "hot sun or autumn frost." The allusion of "standing in the snow to wait upon Master Cheng respectfully" clearly reflects Cheng Yi's teaching style. As for their attitudes toward life, Cheng Hao pursued the realm of life that "integrated with human and things" and paid attention to the self-cultivation of mind and harmony; while Cheng Yi "followed the rituals carefully for many years," and paid more attention to the self-cultivation of "respect" and "investigation of things." There are a few relics and remains about the two Cheng Brothers in Luoyang. The native place of the two Cheng brothers is located at Cheng Village that lies 15 kilometers away from the northeast of Song County, Luoyang. In the Yuan Dynasty, an ancestral temple of the two Cheng

格温和、风趣,与之相处"如坐春风"。程颐则显得严逸、谨慎,讲究师道尊严,对弟子犹如"烈日秋霜"。"程门立雪"的典故很能反映程颐的教学风格。在生活态度方面,大程追求"浑然与物同体"的人生境界,注重"定心""和乐"的修身功夫;小程则"谨于礼四五十年",更为注重"持敬""格物"的修身功夫。洛阳地区今天保存了与二程相关的不少遗迹,二程故里位于嵩县城东北15公里的程村,元代建有二程祠庙,后历代有整修。二程墓在伊川县城西的白虎山下,墓园占地40余亩,前为祠庙,后为墓冢。明代在洛阳西关周公庙东侧建有二程祠、伊洛渊源祠等,经清代重修,至今还保留有部分建筑和碑刻。

宋代以后洛阳出现不少理学名人。明代洛阳地区理学兴盛,学者荟萃,出现了曹端、刘健、尤时熙、孟化鲤等人。清代河洛大儒有耿介等,而思想总体上趋向保守。

brothers was built there and it was refurbished by the later dynasties. At the foot of White Tiger Hill in the west of Yichuan County, there is the cemetery of the two Cheng brothers. The cemetery covers an area of over 40 Mu, comprised of a front ancestral temple and a rear grave. In the Ming Dynasty, the ancestral temple and the original temple of the two Cheng brothers were built in the east of the Duke of Zhou Temple in Xiguan, Luoyang. Nowadays, we can still see reserved architecture and inscriptions that were refurbished in the Qing Dynasty.

Many Neo-Confucian scholars have appeared in Luoyang since the Song Dynasty (960 AD-1279 AD). In the Ming Dynasty (1368 AD-1644 AD), Neo-Confucianism continued to flourish and there were many scholars including Cao Duan, Liu Jian, You Shixi, and Meng Huali and so on. Generally speaking, Neo-Confucian scholars like GengJie were conservative during the Qing Dynasty (1636 AD -1912 AD) in the Heluo region.

第四章

经济科教

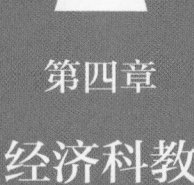

Chapter 4

Economy, Science, Technology, and Education

河洛地区的经济、科技与教育的发展，与其古都文化的兴衰发展交相辉映。河洛地区成为王朝的中央时，由于古都强大的集聚功能，其经济、科技与教育在相当长的历史时期走在中国乃至世界的前列。

一、河洛经济

河洛地区农业历史悠久。《论语》云："禹、稷躬稼而有天下。"夏代中原地区主要是旱作农业，以黍和粟为主。洛阳高崖仰韶文化遗址、皂角树二里头文化遗址都出土了碳化的水稻标本，说明水稻种植在当时已经较为普遍了。此外，二里头遗址中发现了不少石器农具，如石斧、石铲、石刀、石锛、石镰等。还有为数甚多的骨铲、蚌铲、陶刀。另外，在房基、灰坑等处发现了耒痕。由此看来，二里头文化时期，先民们已经进入了耒耜阶段。

"杜康造酒"表明了河洛地区农业的发达。现今洛阳市汝阳县杜康村，传说就是杜康故里，即为杜康酿酒处。二里头遗址中也发现了大量的夏代酒器，包括壶、尊、罍、盉、爵、斝、杯、角等。历史记载商人喜欢饮酒，商纣王嗜酒是其亡国的原因之一。偃师商城内考古发现了窖穴和大量酒器。窖穴内储存的粮食作物主要有禾（粟，小米）、黍、麦、稻、麻，算是当时的"五谷"。酒器主要有爵、斝、觚和盉等，证明当时的粮食生产除了满足人们的正常消耗外，还有多余的粮食用于酿酒。

商代是我国古代商业和商品交换迅速发展的时代。《诗·商颂》载："相土烈烈，海外有截。"相土是商人的第11代祖，他发明了马车，为从事远距离货物贸易提供了便利条件。考古发现偃师商城内设有"市"。《隐居通议》言："古人未有市，若朝聚井汲水，便将货物于井边买卖，故言市井。"说明原始的货物交易场所是"市井"。商代专门的贸易活动，催生了商人阶层的产生。商代人非常重视贝，商王对贵

Economic, scientific, technological, and educational development in the Heluo region changed with the vicissitudes of Luoyang, the ancient capital city. Heluo region stood as the center of different dynasties and thanks to its outstanding function as a gathering place, it ranked top China and even the world in terms of the economy, science, technology, and education for a long historical period.

I. Economy in the Heluo Region

The Heluo region enjoyed a long history of agricultural development. There is a saying in *The Analects*, "Yu and Ji personally wrought at the toils of husbandry, and they became possessors of the Kingdom." Dry land farming of mostly *shu* (broomcorn millet) and millet dominated agriculture on the central plain region in the Xia Dynasty (2070 BC-1600 BC). In Luoyang, carbonized rice samples were unearthed at the sites of Yangshao Culture in Gaoya Village and Erlitou Culture in Zaojiaoshu village, indicating that rice cultivation was quite common at that time. In addition, a great number of farm tools made of stone including zaxes, stone shovels, stone knives, stone adzes, stone sickles, and many shovels made out of bone, clamshell, and ceramic knives were discovered at the sites of Erlitou Culture. People also found tracks of ancient plows at building foundations and ash pits that proved people who lived during the Erlitou Culture period had learned to use plows and plowshares to farm.

The legend of "Du Kang brewing" shows the development of agriculture in the Heluo region. Du Kang Village in Ruyang County, Luoyang City, is reputed because Du Kang came from there and it was there that he brewed. There were also a mass of drinking vessels used in the Xia Dynasty that included kettles, *zun* (an important ancient sacrificial wine-vessel), *lei* (an ancient urn-shaped wooden wine-vessel), *he* (an ancient vessel used for mixing drinks), jue (an ancient wine vessel with three legs and a loop handle), *jia* (an ancient vessel used for warming wine), cups and *jiao* (an ancient vessel used for keeping and pouring wine) that were uncovered at the site of Erlitou Culture. It is documented that people in the Shang Dynasty (1600 BC-1046 BC) liked drinking. The intemperance of King Zhou of the Shang Dynasty has proven to be one of the reasons for Shang's

图4-1 杜康造酒
Figure 4-1 Du Kang, the First Distiller in China

downfall. Archeologists discovered cellars which served as the storage for mainly five cereal types including *he* (millet), *shu*, wheat; rice, and flax at that time, and many drinking vessels at the Shang City site in Yanshi. The unearthed *jue, jia*, *gu* (an ancient horn-shaped drinking vessel with a circle foot, wide mouth, and long body), *he* and other wine vessels testify that the grain output in the Shang Dynasty met daily demand and there was a surplus that was used to brew wine.

Ancient China's commerce and commodity exchange developed rapidly in the Shang Dynasty. A saying in *Hymns of Shang* of *The Book of Songs* goes, "Xiangtu, his martial grandson, ruled over land and sea he had won." As one of the 11th generation ancestors of Shang people, Xiangtu invented coaches and facilitated long-distance trade in goods. Archaeological discoveries proved that there were markets in the Shang City site in Yanshi. The original trading place for goods was *Shijing*. It was recorded that in ancient times, "there were no markets (called *shi* in Chinese). Therefore, people tended to sell their goods at the well (*jing* in Chinese) when fetching water in the morning. That's why we call the market *Shijing*." The merchant class came into existence in the Shang Dynasty as trading increasingly specialized. People, at that time, attached significant importance to shells which were usually given, by the King of Shang, to nobles and courtiers as awards. This showed the high value of shells. It is easy to find that in terms of the structure, most of the Chinese characters related to wealth and value are composed based on the radical 贝, which means "shell" in Chinese.

From the Western Han Dynasty (202 BC-8 AD) and the Eastern Han Dynasty (25 AD-220 AD), the Tianzhuang economy developed significantly because of the expansion, using force, of the landlords. In Luoyang, "hundreds of mansions of rich people are connected one to another, their fertile fields were everywhere in the wild, and slaves, servants and subordinates were in their hundreds." Improvement of iron farm tools in the Han Dynasty (202 BC-220 AD) contributed to the further extension of cultivation technologies. In 1955, a total of 120 iron farm tools including plows, hoes, shovels, sickles, knives, saws, axes, adzes, nails, hammers, hooks, etc. were found in a Eastern Han Dynasty tomb in the western suburbs of Luoyang. At the same time, the significant progress in irrigation technology led to the replacement of the *shuidui* (a machine to husk rice by water power), *fanche* (an agricultural waterwheel), and other

族和臣子的赏赐，最常用的是贝，这说明贝价值很高。在我国汉文字结构中可以看到，凡与财富、价值有关的字，也多以贝为偏旁。

两汉以来，豪强地主势力膨胀，田庄经济有了较大的发展。都城洛阳出现了"豪人之室，连栋数百，膏田满野，奴婢千群，徒附万计"的局面。汉代铁制农具的改进与发展，促使农耕技术得到进一步的推广。1955年在洛阳西郊发掘的东汉墓中发现的铁质工具有犁、锄、铲、镰、刀、锯、斧、锛、钉、锤、勾环等共120件。灌溉技术也得到很大的提高，灌溉辅助工具水碓、翻车的使用也已经超过前期。据《通志》记载，东汉中平三年（186年），由毕岚制造了用于取河水洒路的翻车。马钧在京城洛阳任职时，在前人基础上改良翻车，"令童儿转之，而灌水自覆，更出更入，其巧百倍于常"，使灌溉水平大大提高。

两汉与魏晋南北朝时期，河洛地区水利事业成就卓著。东汉建武二十四年（48年），"穿阳渠，引洛水为漕"，使阳渠满足了漕运的需要，起到了堰洛通槽的效果。阳嘉四年（135年），汉顺帝下诏兴修上东门外漕渠和石桥，再次对阳渠进行整修，使东阳渠中途改道，与洛阳城南的漕运渠道汇合，形成了"东通河济、南引江淮，方贡委输，所由而至"的漕运网络。曹魏时期，筑拦河堰阻断谷水，形成一座横断谷水的石坝，称为"千金堨"，"千金堨"可以增加水量，调节谷水水位，利用水位差引谷水入洛阳城，满足城市内用水，同时可以充当护城河的作用。水利工程的修建，为当时的农业生产、漕运等提供了强有力的保障。

丝绸之路的开通，有力地促进了两汉与魏晋南北朝时期河洛地区的经济繁荣。河洛地区养蚕、丝织业、麻织业有一定的生产规模。据《后汉书·明德马皇后纪》记载，"置织室，蚕于濯龙中"，皇后出于俭朴在都城洛阳的濯龙园中养蚕，设置纺织室。西晋洛阳大富豪石崇、王恺常常争强斗胜，相互攀比，王恺用紫丝巾做四十里步障来显示自己的富有，而"石崇作锦步障五十里以敌之"。石崇与王恺斗富说明洛阳当

auxiliary irrigation tools that were used before. It is mentioned in the *Historical Records* of the later Han dynasty (947 AD-950 AD) that Bi Lan invented the *fanche* that was used to water the roads using river water in the third year of Zhongping in the Eastern Han Dynasty (186 AD). Ma Jun, a famous Chinese inventor in the Three Kingdom period, improved the *fanche* when he served as an official in Luoyang, the capital at that time. He "makes children rotate the *fanche*, the water repeatedly pours unto the ground on its own, turning the car in and out, rendering it a hundred times more ingenious than a normal one," and thus the irrigation level was greatly improved.

Water conservancy in the Heluo region had achieved outstanding achievements during the Western and Eastern Han, Wei, Jin, and Southern and Northern dynasties. In the twenty-fourth year of Jianwu in the Eastern Han Dynasty (48 AD), the "Yang canal was excavated to take advantage of the Luo River in transporting grain." This way, the task of building weirs in the Luo River for grain transporting was accomplished. In the fourth year of Yangjia in the Han Dynasty (135 AD), Emperor Shun issued an imperial edict to construct a canal and stone bridges outside the Shang Dong Gate as well as rebuild the Yang Canal again thereby diverting the east part of the Yang Canal to the grain transporting canal in the southern area of Luoyang City. A grain transporting network of "connecting the Yellow River and the Ji River on the east, diverting the water of the Yangtz River and the Huai River on the south, and transporting all local tributes" was finished. During the Kingdom of Wei period, Qianjin'ai, a great dam transversely breaking water in the valley was built. Its construction led to an increase in the water volume making it possible to adjust the water level in the valley and therefore enable it to flow into Luoyang City for urban water consumption and the moat. With the water conservancy project, agricultural production and grain transporting were considerably guaranteed.

The opening of the Silk Road effectively promoted the economic prosperity of the Heluo region during the Western and Eastern Han, Wei, Jin, and Southern and Northern Dynasties. Sericulture, the silk industry, and the linen industry in the Heluo region had also developed a certain scale of production. According to "Records of Queen Mingde" of *History of the Later Han Dynasty*, "silk weaving mills are set up in Zhuolong Park." The frugal Queen Mingde let people breed

时拥有较大量的丝织品。中西方丝绸之路的开通，成就了洛阳"沟通千城"的国际性商贸都会。东汉洛阳城已有金市、马市等市场，西晋还设立了五谷市作为粮食的交易场所，北魏的大市更是方圆八里，四方物资云集，天下奇珍汇聚，"仅京师洛阳的胡商，就有万余家之多"。

隋唐大运河的贯通，使古都洛阳不仅成为当时的政治中心，更成为经济的重地。隋唐在营建洛阳城的过程中，修建了含嘉仓、子罗仓等许多规模巨大的粮仓。在巩（今巩义市）东南置洛口仓（亦称兴洛仓），"筑仓城，周围二十余里，穿三千窖，窖容八千石以还"。又"置回洛仓于洛阳北七里，仓城周回十里，穿三百窖"。这些仓窖储粮丰富，布帛山积。好大喜功的隋炀帝为了炫耀国富力强，在帝都洛阳的丰都市大讲排场，"胡客或过酒食店，悉令邀延就坐，醉饱而散，不取其直，给之曰：'中国丰饶，酒食例不取直。'胡客皆惊叹"。盛唐时期，农业连年丰收，粮价便宜。杜甫《忆昔》诗曰："忆昔开元全盛日，小邑犹藏万家室。稻米流脂粟米白，公私仓廪俱丰实"。此外，洛阳的冶铸业技艺高超，武则天时铸成的铜鼎天枢精妙绝伦，在洛阳墓葬中出土了大量的花纹图饰精美的铜镜，工艺非同凡响。

隋唐时期古都洛阳不仅成为全国水陆交通的中枢之地，而且成为天下货物集散地和全国经济、物资交流的中心。《隋书》记载："每岁正月，万国来朝，留至十五日"，"百官起棚夹路，从昏达旦"，"一万八千人大列炬火，光烛天地"。这些文字反映了隋代古都洛阳作为国际贸易都会的盛况。唐代为适应经济和商业发展的需要，在洛阳城内构建了以洛水为中枢的漕运交通，北岸有漕渠、瀍水、泄城渠，还有立德坊和武则天时期开凿的当时最大的停泊区新潭。新潭是大运河在都城洛阳的漕运码头。"天下之舟船所集，常万余艘，填满河路，商旅贸易，车马填塞"。"弘舸巨舰，千舳万艘，交贸往还，昧旦永日"，大批货物运进转出，大批客商云集，洛阳实际上成为全国乃至国际商贸的集散中心、天下富商大贾汇集之地。

silkworms in Zhuolong Park in the capital, Luoyang City. Shi Chong and Wang Kai were famous millionaires in Luoyang in the West Jin Dynasty (226 AD-316 AD) and they competed against each other for everything. For example, if Wang Kai made a 20 kilometer-long screen along the road with purple silk scarves to show off his wealth, "Shi Chong made one too to compete." The competition between Shi Chong and Wang Kai shows that there was plenty of silk fabric in Luoyang at that time. The Silk Road connecting China and the West transformed Luoyang into an international commerce and trade capital "communicating thousand of cities." In the Eastern Han Dynasty, there had already been the Golden market (the market specializing in international trade), the horse market, and other markets in Luoyang. A "Five Cereal" market was opened for grain transactions in the Western Jin Dynasty. The Great Market in the Northern Wei Dynasty (386 AD-534 AD), covering an area of 16 square kilometers, was a gathering for a large number and variety of goods from different areas.

The connection of China's Grand Canal of the Sui-Tang Dynasty (581 AD-907 AD) enabled Luoyang to become the current political capital and economic highland. When constructing Luoyang City in Sui and Tang dynasties, people set up many large granaries like Hanjia Granary and Ziluo Granary. Luokou Granary (also called Xingluo Granary) was built in the southeast of Gong County (present-day Gongyi City). Around Luokou granary, a fort was built that had a 10 kilometer-long wall, and about 3000 storage vaults were dug. Approximately 3 kilometers north of the city, Huiluo granary, with 300 storage vaults, was built within a fort that measured 5 kilometers in circumference. These granaries were rich in grain storage, and the cloth and silk were accumulated into mountains. In order to flaunt the great wealth and strength of the Sui Dynasty (581 AD-618 AD), the arrogant and flatulent Emperor Yang organized such an ostentatious banquet at Fengdu Market in Luoyang that "all foreign guests who pass near restaurants are invited to attend the banquet, glutting themselves with delicacies and wine for free, and were made to believe that 'China is rich and fertile to the extent that people needn't pay for food and wine.' The foreign guests were greatly surprised." During the heyday of the Tang Dynasty (618 AD-907 AD), people had bumper harvests year after year, so the price of food was cheap. As is described in a poem by Du Fu, one of the greatest poets in Chinese history, "In

图4-2　隋唐洛阳城定鼎门
Figure 4-2　Dingding Gate in Sui and Tang Dynasties

the prosperous time of the period of Kai Yuan, even a small country city would be crowded with the rich; rice flowed like oil and both public and private granaries were stuffed with grain." In addition, the metallurgy industry was developed and metallurgical technologies reached an excellent level. The bronze tripod and *tianshu* (the world's central hub according to the people of that time) built during the reign of Empress Wu Zetian were rather exquisite and outstanding. The multitudes of bronze mirrors unearthed in the tombs of Luoyang were all embellished with elegant patterns and were an embodiment of extraordinary craftsmanship.

Luoyang, the ancient capital of the Sui and Tang dynasties was the pivot of China's land and water communication, an excellent distribution center, and even the center of the national economy and commodities. A saying in *The Book of the Sui Dynasty* goes, "in the first month of the lunar year each year, countries all over the world send ambassadors to pay tributes to China. The ambassadors do not leave until January fifteenth of the lunar year…In this course, officials of the Chinese court dawn to dusk construct sheds on the two sides of the streets… Numerous people erect torches which are so bright that the whole world is illuminated." This reflected the spectacular scene of Luoyang, the capital city of the Sui Dynasty, as the capital of international trade. People constructed the grain transporting network centered on the Luo River as a result of the economic and commercial development that had taken place. In the north bank stood Cao Canal, Chan River, Xie Cheng Canal, Li De Fang as well as Xin Tan, the largest wharf at that time which was built during the period of Empress Wu Zetian. Xin Tan was the wharf of the Great Canal in Luoyang City. "It's common for people to see the prosperous scene that shows an assembly of over ten thousand coaches and ships from around the country swarming on the road and river. Coaches and horses of businessmen caused congestion…Thousands of fleets of huge ships come and go as they carry goods all the time, even late into the night, and just as busy as they are during the daytime." Here, swarms of traveling traders gathered, and multitudes of goods were exported and imported transforming Luoyang into a hub for China's rich people and an actual distribution center of national and even international commerce and trade.

北宋时期，洛阳作为西京经济有所恢复，官僚士大夫也普遍在此兴修宅第园林。北宋末年到元代的100余年中，河洛地区历经战火，不仅使经济生产无法恢复，兵燹之下人口也大量减少，而有财资者则大批南迁。明中期以后，随着大量荒芜的土地得到开垦，农业经济得以恢复并得到发展，这从关林庙会、白马寺庙会等可见一斑。清代在洛阳经商者大多为外地商人，"盐、当各商多晋人"。洛阳城内有两处会馆，即山陕会馆和潞泽会馆，均为乾隆年间来洛山陕商人所建。总体来看，元明清时期，河洛经济呈现衰落之势，历史辉煌已"无可奈何花落去"。

As the western capital, Luoyang, to a certain extent, made progress in economic recovery in the Northern Song Dynasty (960 AD-1127 AD). Bureaucrats and scholar-officials tended to build residences and parks in Luoyang. During the more than 100 years from the end of the North Song Dynasty to the Yuan Dynasty (1271 AD-1368 AD), the Heluo region suffered incessant wars which prevented economic recovery, caused mass casualties, and gave rise to the wholesale migration of wealthy people southward. After the mid-Ming Dynasty, with the cultivation of a large amount of barren land, the agricultural economy was restored and developed as evidenced by the Guanlin Temple Fair and the White Horse Temple Fair. Most of the businessmen in Luoyang were not local people. " Businessmen trading in salt and pawn at large came from Shanxi." Both the two guild halls——Shanxi & Shaanxi Guildhall and Luze Guildhall in Luoyang City were established by Shanxi and Shaanxi businessmen who came to Luoyang during the reign of Emperor Qianlong. On the whole, the Heluo economy gradually declined from the Yuan, Ming, and Qing dynasties. Just as Yan Shu, a famous poet, said "Nothing can be done about flowers falling away," so nothing could be done about the glorious history of the Heluo economy.

二、河洛科技

河洛地区的科学技术，在天文历法、陶瓷制造、金属铸造、医学、造纸和印刷、机械制造、建筑雕塑、农业技术等方面源远流长，曾涌现出许许多多的科学巨子，在中国乃至世界科技史上占有重要地位。

河洛地区的天文历法

人类自诞生之始便与日月星辰为伴，进入农耕社会后更是离不开对日月星辰运行的观测。《夏小正》最早载于汉代的《大戴礼记》，相传它是夏代的历法。西周初期的"周公测影"法，是用圭表测日影的方法确定节气的，并进步到能确定"朔日"。秦汉时期河洛地区天文学家的典型代表是张衡。其《浑天仪图注》全面总结和论述了浑天说的理论，这是以地球为中心的宇宙观。他于公元132年在洛阳首创世界上第一架地震仪即"地动仪"，并准确地记录了公元138年发生在甘肃的强震。

唐代的僧一行在洛阳制成了以漏水转动的浑天铜仪。铜仪上的两个木人，一个每刻一击鼓，一个每时辰一撞钟，这是世界上较为完善的最早的机械自动计时器，也称机械天文钟。他还组织了一次大规模的天文测量，测出了二十八宿距天球北极的度数，在世界上第一次发现了恒星位置变化的现象，比英国人哈雷发现恒星移动几乎早千年。僧一行在历法方面的成就是花费六七年时间修订了《大衍历》，这是当时世界上最先进的历法。元代天文学家郭守敬在登封告成镇（古称阳城）建造了观星台，并编制颁布了新历《授时历》。告成镇的观星台，是我国现存最早的天文台建筑。2010年8月1日，包含观星台在内的登封"天地之中"历史建筑群被列为世界文化遗产。

河洛地区的金属铸造

青铜器的出现，对提高社会生产力起到了划时代的作用。偃师二里头夏文化遗存丰富，出土和搜集的铜器有二百余件，其中出土的铜爵，

II. Science and Technology in the Heluo Region

In the Heluo region, science and technology in astronomy, calendars, ceramics, metal casting, medicine, paper-making, printing, machine manufacturing, architecture, sculpture, and agriculture were crucial and they occupied the pole position in the history of science and technology in China and even the world.

Astronomy and calendars in the Heluo region

The moon and stars have accompanied mankind from time immemorial. Stepping into an agricultural society, mankind simply relied essentially on the movement of the sun, moon, and stars. It is said that *Xia Xiaozheng*, which was firstly recorded in *The Record of Rites by Dai the Elder* of the Han Dynasty, became the calendar of the Xia Dynasty. The Zhou Gong Measuring Shadow method of the early period of the Western Zhou Dynasty (1046 BC-771 BC) was adopted to ascertain solar terms by measuring the shadow using gnomons. People had made so much progress that they were able to determine the first day of the lunar month. Zhang Heng was the typical representative astronomer of the Heluo region in the Qin and Han dynasties. His *Annotation to the Armillary Sphere* comprehensively summarized and discussed the theory of sphere-heavens, which was an earth-centric view of the universe. In 132 AD in Luoyang, he was the first to invent the world's first seismograph, namely the tellurion, and was able to obtain an exact recording of the strong shock in Gansu Province in 138 AD.

Seng Yixing of the Tang Dynasty successfully made a bronze tellurion powered by water power in Luoyang. It's also the earliest mechanical automatic timer——mechanical chronometer, on which two puppets were set, one drummed once every fifteen minutes and the other, every two hours. Yixing still organized large-scale astronomic surveying. He measured degrees of the lunar mansions to the north pole of the celestial sphere and, nearly a thousand years earlier than British Halley, led the world in the discovery of positional changes of fixed stars. In terms of the calendar, he spent six or seven years formulating the world's most advanced calendar at that time—the Dayan Calendar. By the time of the Yuan Dynasty, Guo Shoujing, a well-known astronomer, constructed a stellar observatory in Gaocheng Town (then known as Yangcheng City), Dengfeng City,

图4-3 张衡地动仪

Figure 4-3　The Seismometer invented by Zhang Heng (AD 78–139)

compiled and promulgated a new calendar—the Shoushi Calendar. The stellar observatory in Gaocheng Town is the earliest existing astronomical observatory in China. On August 1st, 2010, Dengfeng's Center of the World historical buildings, including the stellar observatory, were listed as a World Cultural Heritage.

Metal casting in the Heluo region

The emergence of bronze wares played an epoch-making role in the improvement of social productive forces. Abundant relics, including more than two hundred bronze wares, were unearthed and collected in the Erlitou cultural heritage of the Xia Dynasty in Yanshi, Henan. A bronze *jue* (ancient wine vessel) unearthed there was hailed as "the first *Jue* of China." Back in the Eastern Zhou Dynasty (770 BC-256 BC), there were iron casting ruins discovered in the Heluo region. A large number and scale of iron smelting workshops accomplished technological progress that translated into the production of a great variety of bronze wares.

Paper-making and printing technologies in the Heluo region

One of the four great scientific and technological inventions of ancient China, paper-making technology, represents the great contribution of China to world civilization. When Cailun, the inventor of papermaking technology, took the position of Shangfang ling at the court in Luoyang during the the Eastern Han Dynasty, he was made responsible for the manufacturing of implements for the emperor, so he undertook revolutionary improvements in papermaking materials and methods. His innovation led to paper mass production, spread, and popularization. Nowadays, in the southeast of a city relic of the Han and Wei Dynasties, there are villages such as Front Paper Village and Back Paper Village. The Papermaking River, with the signal "Papermaking River Site" on its bank, runs on the northeast of Gou's Town in Yanshi, and it is said to be the place where Cai Lun made paper.

Medicine in the Heluo region

With a group of noted doctors and medical works, the Heluo region became an area of great importance during the formation and development of Chinese traditional medicine. Hua Tuo, in the period of Three Kingdoms, was the world's first medical scientist to use anesthetics in operations. He invented anesthesia powder in Luoyang, making a significant contribution to China's medical

被誉为"中华第一爵"。东周时期,河洛地区已经发现有铸铁遗址,到了秦汉冶铁作坊多、规模更大,技术更高,出产的器型更加丰富。

河洛地区的造纸术和印刷术

造纸术是中国古代科学技术的四大发明之一,是中国对于世界文明的伟大贡献。蔡伦在东汉洛阳宫廷任主管制造御用器物的尚方令,他对造纸在原料和方法上都进行了革命性的改造,使纸的大量生产成为可能,为纸的推广和普及开辟了广阔道路。在汉魏故城东南,今有前纸庄、后纸庄等村落,在偃师缑氏镇东北有造纸河,岸边立有"造纸河遗址"标志,相传均为当年蔡伦造纸之地。

河洛地区的医学

河洛地区是中医形成和发展的重要地区,出现一批名医和医学著作。三国时期的华佗是世界上最早使用麻醉剂进行手术的医学家。他在洛阳发明的麻沸散为中国的医学事业做出了重大贡献。魏晋时期的王叔和,在洛阳帝都任太医令,编撰《脉经》10卷,这是世界上现存最早的脉学专著。唐朝洛阳名医张文仲,在唐高宗和武则天时是宫廷内擅长"风疾"治疗的御医,他为后人留下的《随身备急方》,是关于治疗风疾的理论和实践在中国医学史上独树一帜,丰富和发展了祖国的医学宝库。

development. The ten volumes of *Pulse Classics*, written by Wang Shuhe when he was the Director of the Imperial Medical Bureau in Luoyang, the capital city, during the period of the Wei and Jin dynasties, are the existing earliest sphygmology monograph. Zhang Wenzhong, the famous Luoyang physician, was an imperial physician quite good at treating stroke during the reign of Emporer Gaozong and Empress Wu Zetian. Theories and practices about stroke treatment in his legacy *Suishen Beiji Prescription* played an outstanding role in the history of Chinese medicine.

三、河洛教育

中国教育的源头可追溯至夏代。关于学校的设置，《孟子·滕文公上》说："设为庠序学校以教之。庠者，养也。校者，教也。序者，射也。夏曰校，殷曰序，周曰庠。学则三代共之，皆所以明人伦也。"春秋战国时期，官学衰落，学术下移，私学在河洛地区逐渐兴起，为教育走向民间做出了贡献。

东汉太学

太学是汉代出现的设在京师的全国最高教育机构，是我国古代最早的大学。西汉武帝时在首都长安最早设立太学。当东汉刘秀称帝后，在建武五年（公元29年）十月，于洛阳城东南的开阳门外兴建太学，四方学士云集京师，于是立五经博士，所招学生称为太学生。后来汉明帝刘庄还到太学行礼讲经。至汉质帝时，太学生人数多至三万人。洛阳太学鼎盛于东汉，其后经曹魏、西晋，至北朝末衰落，历时六七百年，是屹立在世界东方的第一所国立中央大学，堪称我国教育史上的奇葩。

唐代科举

科举制度不仅对中国文化教育影响深远，而且也影响中国政治生活长达一千余年。科举制创始于隋，完成于唐。唐高宗驻守洛阳的时间累计十一年，洛阳的科举活动开始活跃起来。上元元年（674年）皇后武则天建议明经科按照策问《孝经》《论语》的办法，加试《老子》。次年初高宗批准，并且令进士科也加试《老子》策问。虽然武则天建周后取消这一做法，但唐玄宗又将其发展成为道举，可见洛阳对此事的奠基作用。调露二年（680年）唐高宗决定明经、进士一律加试帖经，此后遂成为制度。因此科举制一些做法的创立成型，与洛阳有关。武则天时期，把科举活动和执政柄、革唐命紧密结合起来，以察舆论。载初元年（689年），各地近万人来洛阳应制举，武则天到城南门楼亲自临试。

III. Education in the Heluo Region

Education in China dates back to the Xia Dynasty. It is recorded in *The Book of Master Meng* that "Schools, *xiang*, *xu*, and *xiao* by name, should be established to educate the people. The name *xiang* means nourishing; *xiao* means teaching; *xu* means archery training. A school in the Xia Dynasty was named *xiao*; in the Yin Dynasty, it was named *xu*; and in the Zhou Dynasty, it was named *xiang*. It is worthy of note that the name *xue* was used by all three dynasties. The purpose of all such schools was to make the learners understand ethical relations." During the Spring and Autumn period, official schools declined, academic activities were no longer a privilege of the upper class, thereby giving the common people an opportunity to attend schools. Private schools were gradually established in the Heluo region, contributing a lot to the vulgarization of education.

Taixue in the Eastern Han Dynasty

Taixue, the imperial academy, was the highest national educational institute established in the capital of the Han Dynasty and it was China's earliest university. Emperor Wu of the Western Han Dynasty was the first to set up Taixue in the capital Chang'an. After Liu Xiu became the emperor of the Eastern Han Dynasty, in October of the fifth year of Jianwu (29 AD), he instituted Taixue outside Kaiyang Gate in the southeast of Luoyang City. Scholars from various regions thus met there. Furthermore, there was the setting up of the Five Classics Doctorate whose students were Tai Student. Afterward, Emperor Ming (Liu Zhuang) came to Taixue to perform the rites of Li and interpret the Five Classics of Confucianism. Up until the reign of Emperor Zhi, Taixue had enrolled as many as 30,000 students. Taixue of Luoyang reached its peak in the Eastern Han Dynasty, went through the Kingdom of Wei under the throne of Caos and the West Jin Dynasty, and faded at the end of the Northern Dynasty (420 AD-589 AD). It was the first national central university in the East, lasting for six or seven hundred years, and has been termed a miracle in China's education history.

The Imperial Civil Examination System of the Tang Dynasty

The Imperial Civil Examination System has exerted a profound influence on not only China's culture and education but also China's politics for over one

她还在洛城殿策问贡士，数日才完毕，开贡士殿试的先河。长安二年（702年）武则天首创武举，考试科目有马射、步射、平射、马枪、负重等。唐玄宗、唐代宗、五代及北宋，河洛地区的洛阳、开封帝都多次举行科举活动。中国有"学而优则仕"的传统，科举在很大程度上规定着天下学子的人生方向和价值追求，也导演了读书人的喜怒哀乐和得失进退。

宋代书院

宋代有四大著名书院，分别是应天府书院（河南商丘）、嵩阳书院（河南登封）、岳麓书院（湖南长沙）、白鹿洞书院（江西九江）。嵩阳书院因坐落在嵩山之阳而得名。宋初，国内太平，文风四起，儒生经五代久乱之后，都喜欢在山林中找个安静的地方聚众讲学。因登封是尧、舜、禹、周公等曾经居住过的地方，宋仁宗景祐二年（1035年）在此建立了嵩阳书院。据记载，先后在嵩阳书院讲学的有范仲淹、司马光、程颢、程颐、杨时、朱熹、李纲、范纯仁等二十四人，司马光的巨著《资治通鉴》第9卷至第21卷就是在嵩阳书院和崇福宫完成的。程颐、程颢在嵩阳书院讲学10余年，这使该书院成为宋代理学的发源地之一。嵩阳书院因其独特的儒学教育建筑性质，被称为研究中国古代书院建筑、教育制度以及儒家文化的标本。2010年8月，嵩阳书院作为"登封'天地之中'历史建筑群"的子项目，被联合国教科文组织正式列入世界文化遗产名录。

元明清时期，因帝都不在河洛地区，这里没有中央一级的学府，只有路、府、州、县四级官学，但并不普及。书院依旧发达，洛阳知名书院有同文书院、伊川书院、洛中书院等。知名的有二程书院、洛中书院等。总体而言，这一时期的河洛地区教育辉煌不在，与沿海和江南相比已远远落后。

thousand years. Budding in the Sui Dynasty, the Imperial Civil Examination System took shape in the Tang Dynasty. For eleven years Emperor Gao Zong of the Tang Dynasty stayed in Luoyang animating Imperial Civil Examination activities in Luoyang. Empress Wu Zetian suggested questions as part of the contents of *The Book of Filial Piety*, *The Analects*, as well as the additional *The Book of Master Lao* in the Ming Jing examination in 647 AD, the first year of Shangyuan (one of the reign titles of emperor Gao Zong). At the beginning of the following year, Gao Zong authorized her suggestion and further added *The Book of Master Lao* into the *Jin Shi* examination. After Wu Zetian ascended the throne, she canceled the rule, while Emperor Xuan Zong developed it into *Tao Ju* (an examination subject that tested Taoist knowledge). Luoyang was the capital city of Wu's reign, so we can see the foundation role Luoyang played in it. In the second year of Diao Lu (one of the reign titles of Gao Zong), Gao Zong decided to take an additional test of *Tie Jing* in both the *Ming Jing* and *Jin Shi* examinations, which became a rule later. Thus, Luoyang had an impact on the creation of some rules of the Imperial Civil Examination System. Wu Zetian gained popular support and a favorable public opinion by combining the Imperial Civil Examination with state power holding and by changing the name of the country. In the first year of Zaichu (690 AD), nearly 10,000 people from all over the world came to Luoyang to take the examination, and Wu Zetian went to the south gate of the city to inspect it. She also questioned *Gong Shi* (candidates who had passed the examination) at Luo City Hall for several days, setting a precedent for the Palace Examination of the final imperial examination. In the second year of Chang' an (702 AD), she began by instituting *Wu Ju*, the imperial examination of military knowledge and skill. Subjects tested in *Wu Ju* included horse-riding archery, walking archery, static archery, horse spear, wrestling with weight, and others. The Imperial Civil Examinations were held in the capital cities of Luoyang and Kaifeng during the reigns of Emperors Xuan Zong and Dai Zong of the Tang Dynasty, the Five Dynasties, and the Northern Song Dynasty. It was a tradition that officialdom is the natural outlet for good scholars in China. The Imperial Civil Examination System, to a large extent, dictated the path of life and the pursuit of value of Chinese scholars and determined their emotions and success in life.

图4-4　嵩阳书院　刘龙/摄
Figure 4-4　Songyang Academy (in Dengfeng, Henan)　Photo by Liu Long

Academies in Song Dynasty (960 AD-1279 AD)

There were four great academies in the Song Dynasty—Yingtian Fu Academy (in Shangqiu, Henan), Songyang Academy (in Dengfeng, Henan), Yuelu Academy (in Changsha, Hunan), and Bailu Dong Academy (in Jiujiang, Jiangxi). The Songyang Academy was so named because of its location on the southern side of Songshan Mountain. At the beginning of the Song Dynasty, people lived in peace, enjoying flourishing academic activities. Confucians, enduring the long-term turmoil of the Five Dynasties, tended to gather in the quiet and wooded mountain to discourse on academic subjects. Because Yao, Sun, Yu, and Zhou Gong had lived in Dengfeng, in the second year of Jing Hu (1035 AD), Emperor Ren Zong of the Song Dynasty constructed the Songyang Academy. It is recorded that twenty-four scholars including Fan Zhongyan, Sima Guang, Cheng Hao, Cheng Yi, Yang Shi, Zhu Xi, Li Gang, and Fan Chunren gave lectures there. In addition, the ninth to twenty-first volumes of *Comprehensive Mirror for Aid in Government*, a monumental work written by Sima Guang, was finished in Songyang Academy and Chongfu palace. Cheng Yi and Cheng Hao taught and delivered lectures in the Academy for over ten years making the academy one of the birthplaces of Neo-Confucianism of the Song Dynasty. As a unique Confucian education architecture , the Songyang Academy has been considered the ideal sample for studying ancient Chinese academy building, education system, and Confucian culture. In August 2010, it was officially listed on UNESCO's World Heritage List as a sub-project of the "Center of The World's Historic Architectures in Dengfeng".

However, the capital city of the Yan, Ming, and Qing Dynasties was situated in Beijing instead of Luoyang, so at that moment, there were no central learning institutions, just the four-level official schools of Lu (an ancient administrative unit), Fu (an ancient administrative unit), province, and county. Besides, the official schools were not generalized. The academies were still well developed, among them were some famous ones, such as Tong Wen Academy, Yi Chuan Academy and Luo Zhong Academy. In general, education in the Heluo region in the Yuan, Ming, and Qing Dynasties was not as glorious as ever before and lagged far behind that in the coast and regions south of the Yangtze River.

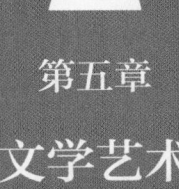

第五章

文学艺术

Chapter 5

Literature and Art

文学艺术包括文学和艺术两个概念。河洛地区在文学、书法、绘画、雕塑、音乐、舞蹈、戏曲等方面都取得了卓越成就，可谓绚丽多彩。

一、河洛文学

以洛阳为中心的河洛地区，是中国古典文学的发祥地，又是其发展演变的关键地区，一部河洛文学史可以说就是一部浓缩了的中国文学史。

先秦河洛文学对整个中国文学具有奠基意义。今存的河洛地区上古歌谣，著名的有《击壤歌》《康衢谣》等。《山海经》是保留上古神话最为丰富的典籍，洛神、河伯、青要之女、愚公移山、夸父逐日、鲧禹治水等故事都与河洛地区相关。《诗经》是我国的第一部诗歌总集，其《国风·周南》《王风》等一些诗篇属于河洛文学。历史散文《尚书》中的虞、夏书各二篇，商书五篇，以及《逸周书》，皆记载河洛地区的历史人物及事件。河洛诸子散文中，老子的《道德经》对后世文学产生了极大的影响。

汉代河洛文学以"赋"为代表。贾谊被称为"洛阳才子"，是著名的赋家。《吊屈原赋》借鉴了楚辞的某些手法，在一定程度上体现出南北文化的融合。《鵩鸟赋》是汉代第一篇散体赋，也是中国早期古典文学作品中生命意识最为强烈的作品之一，其主客问答的形式成为后来赋体文学的一大传统。班固《两都赋》先颂扬光武帝的建国伟业，继述明帝修洛邑，再说田猎、宴饮、祭祀的盛况，以显示东汉洛阳帝都的声威，成为汉代都城赋的开端之作。张衡《二京赋》描写了长安、洛阳繁华热闹的街道市场、杂技歌舞及各色人等，被称为"汉代散体大赋的绝响"。《古诗十九首》在中国诗史上被誉为"五言之冠冕"，可以确定产生于洛阳的诗歌就有《青青陵上柏》《驱车上东门》等数首。班固在

Literature and art can be divided into the concept of literature and the concept of art. The Heluo region has made outstanding achievements in literature, calligraphy, painting, sculpture, music, dance, opera, and other aspects that can be described as enjoying brilliant literature and art atmosphere.

I . Literature in the Heluo Region

The Heluo region, centered in Luoyang, is the birthplace of classical Chinese literature and a pivotal area for development of the classical Chinese literature. The history of Heluo literature epitomizes the history of Chinese literature.

Heluo literature of the pre-Qin period (351 AD-394 AD) laid the foundation for the entire Chinese literature. Some ancient songs of the Heluo region including the famous *Ode for Beating the Land (Ji Rang Ge)* and *Song of Kangqu (Kang Qu Yao)* have survived till date. Numerous stories in *Shan Hai Jing*, the classic containing the most colorful ancient fairy tales, were relevant to the Heluo region. For example, Goddess of the Luo River, God of the Luo River, Daughter of Qingyao, Yu Gong Moving Mountains, Kuafu Chasing the Sun, Kun and Yu Taming the Flood, and others.*The Book of Songs* is China's first poetry collection. The Songs Collected South of the Capital of Modern Shaanxi and Henan,Songs Collected around the Capital were collected from the Heluo region. In *The Book of History*, two texts of "Book of Yu" and "Book of Xia", and five texts of "Book of Shang" all record events and life around Luoyang. The *Tao Te Ching* written by Lao Tzu has exerted great influence on later literature.

Ode (an ancient Chinese literary genre) is representative of Heluo literature in the Han Dynasty. Jia Yi, also known as "The talent of Luoyang," was a renowned ode writer. Some writing techniques of *Ode to Qu Yuan* were drawn in *Chu Ci (Ode of Chu)*, displaying the fusion of North and South cultures. *Ode to the Giant Peng Bird* was the first prose ode in the Han Dynasty, and it was also one of the works with the strongest sense of life in early Chinese classical literature. The form of the question and the answer became a great tradition in later ode literature.*Liang Du Ode*,written by Ban Gu, was the start of odes to the capital in the Han Dynasty. The ode began by praising the great work of Emperor Guang Wu of the Han Dynasty then the rebuilding of Luoyang by Emperor

洛阳完成了中国第一部纪传体断代史《汉书》，开辟了不同于《史记》的艺术风貌。

魏晋南北朝时局动荡，而河洛文学呈现出繁荣之势。建安文学代表作家在洛阳创作了大量优秀的作品，如曹操的《薤露行》、曹植的《送应氏》《洛神赋》、曹丕的《典论·论文》、蔡琰的《悲愤诗》等。正始文学的代表人物"竹林七贤"主要活动在洛阳帝都一带，其中的山涛、向秀皆是河洛本土作家。西晋时期在洛阳形成了一个著名的文人集团"金谷二十四友"，他们经常在金谷园中饮酒作诗，其存诗占了西晋文人诗歌的一半。左思在洛阳创作了著名的《三都赋》，一时间"豪贵之家，竞相传写，洛阳为之纸贵"（《晋书·左思传》）。北朝河洛文学的代表作品是杨衒之的《洛阳伽蓝记》，对洛阳"城郭崩毁，宫室倾覆，寺观灰烬，庙塔丘墟"的叙述，充满了黍离之悲。

唐代是河洛文学的巅峰时期。初唐高宗及武后之世在洛阳形成了"北门学士""珠英学士"两个庞大的宫廷文人集团。中唐新乐府运动，以白居易、元稹为领袖。白居易在洛阳生活了二十多年，讴歌洛阳的诗作有《上阳白发人》《洛城东花下作》《中隐》《开龙门八节滩》等800多首。白居易经常与东都文人刘禹锡、令狐楚、李德裕、裴度等诗酒唱和，组建"香山九老会"，以洛阳为"中隐"之地，吟玩性情、知足常乐，这种人生态度为后世诗人所崇尚，苏轼尤其倾倒。后人遂将这种生活方式称为"白苏风流"。李贺是福昌（今河南宜阳）人，诗歌想象奇特，用语奇倔，使他获得了"诗鬼"的称号。晚唐李商隐是怀州河内（今沁阳）人，他"虚负凌云万丈才，一生襟抱未曾开"，遭受牛、李两党的倾轧而受尽排挤和责难，辗转于藩镇幕府天涯漂泊，其时事诗忧国愤世，言志诗苦闷感伤，爱情诗绵邈深沉。

唐代河洛文学的代表作家是杜甫。杜甫的青少年时代是在洛阳度过的。25岁他游伊阙龙门，写下"阴壑生虚籁，月林散清影。天阙象纬逼，云卧衣裳冷"的名句，而《龙门》则描写了东都佛寺的盛况。他在

Ming was narrated, and, at last, a spectacular scene of hunting, attending banquets, and offering sacrifice was described to show the grand prestige of Luoyang as the capital of the East Han Dynasty. In Zhang Heng's *Ode to Er Jing*, bustling streets and markets, acrobatic, singing and dancing performances, and various kinds of people were depicted. The ode achieved the title of the "culmination of prosaic odes of the Han Dynasty." In the history of Chinese poetry, *Nineteen Ancient Poems* was hailed as the "crown of five character poetry." We could make sure that many poems like *Green, Green, the Cypress on the Bridge* and *I Drive My Carriage from the Upper East Gate* were created in Luoyang. It was in Luoyang that Ban Gu finished *History of the Han Dynasty*, China's first biographic dynastic history book, opening up an artistic style different from that of The Records of the Historian.

The time in the Wei, Jin, Northern, and Southern dynasties, when Heluo literature saw its prosperous development, was one of uncertainty. Representative writers of Jian'an Literature created a large number of excellent works in Luoyang including Cao Cao's *Xie Lu Xing*, Cao Zhi's *Farewell to Ying Shi*, and *Ode to Luo Goddess*, Cao Pi's *Thesis of Classic Theory*, Cai Yan's *Poems of Grief and Angry*. The representative scholars of Zhengshi Literature, "Seven Sages of the Bamboo Forest," among whom Shan Tao and Xiang Xiu are both Luoyang native writers, mainly worked in the Luoyang imperial capital area. A well-known literati group—"Twenty-Four Friends of Jingu Garden" came into being in Luoyang in the Western Jin Dynasty. Literati of the group used to drink and write poems in Jingu Garden, leaving behind so many poems that occupy half of the literati poetry of the Western Jin Dynasty. It was also in Luoyang that Zuo Si created *San Du Ode* which, at one time, led to the fact that "rich people competed so intensively to transcribe that the paper price in Luoyang went up" ("Biography of Zuo Si" in *The Book of the Jin Dynasty*). Yang Xuanzhi was the representative of the literature of the Heluo region. *His Record of Buddhist Temples* in Luoyang depicts a scene where "the Luoyang City collapses, palaces topple, temples are burning, towers get ruined," disclosing the sorrow of the country's dilapidation and the loss of home.

The Tang Dynasty was the peak literature of the Heluo region. Two large royal literati groups, Beimen Scholar and Zhuying Scholar, were formed in

图5-1 李贺
Figure 5-1 Li He

洛阳曾经听到宫廷乐师李龟年的歌唱,由此也留下了晚年"落花时节又逢君"的慨叹。杜甫在长安求仕期间,也有多次回洛阳的探家之旅,期间以新题乐府的形式写下的"三吏""三别",达到了现实主义的诗歌创作高峰。盛世东都的生活和文化奠定了他以儒家"修齐治平"为目标的入世情怀,陶冶了他风雅正宗的诗歌审美情趣。

唐代河洛文学不可忽略的还有游洛、寓洛的作家,如李白、王维、孟浩然、岑参、孟郊等,他们都留下了书写河洛山川风物的佳作。伟大的浪漫主义诗人李白在天宝年间曾多次来到洛阳,也曾短期在嵩山隐居,其《洛城闻笛》《天津秋》等皆已成为千古传颂的名作。天宝三年(744年),李白与杜甫在洛阳相会,"醉眠秋共被,携手日同行"(杜甫《与李十二白同寻范十隐居》),从此结下了深厚的友谊,成为文学史上的千秋佳话。

宋代河洛文学亦是大家云集。欧阳修在洛阳西京四年期间与富弼等人结为诗友,形成了著名的西京幕府文人集团,使洛阳成为当时全国诗文创作中心和诗文革新运动的发祥地。欧阳修的《洛阳牡丹记》叙花

Luoyang during the reigns of Emperor Gao Zong and Empress Wu Zetian at the beginning of the Tang Dynasty. Up until the middle of the Tang Dynasty, Ba Juyi and Yuanchen became leaders of the New Yue Fu Movement, a poetic innovation movement. Having lived in Luoyang for more than twenty years, Baijuyi wrote over 800 poems to eulogize Luoyang. For example, *Shangyang White-Headed Elders*, *Poem Sung Among Flowers in Eastern Luoyang*, *An Average Hermit*, *Removing the Eight Pebble Beaches New Longmen*, and others. He also drank, versified, and made responsory poems in the eastern capital, Luoyang, together with other scholars including Liu Yuxi, Ling Huchu, Li Deyu, and Pei Du. He also assembled a literati group named "Union of Nine Elders of Xiangshan Mountain" that took Luoyang as the site of their average hermit where they amused themselves to their hearts' content. Their behavior became customary among later poets particularly Su Shi, and was called "Bai Su Romance."Born in Fuchang (present-day Yiyang, Henan Province), Li He gained the title of "Ghost of Poetry" due to his fancy imagination and peculiar wording. In the late Tang Dynasty (923 AD-936 AD), Li Shangyin was a native of Hanei of Huaizhou (present-day Qinyang). He was "a man of great talent who remained unrecognized and who failed to achieve his ambition." He was sidelined and condemned by the two parties of Niu and Li and had to live on the patronage of different military governors and warlords. In his poems on politics, he worried about the country and the resentment against the time. In the poems expressing aspiration, he showed sorrow and depression. In love poems, he thought meticulously and deeply.

  Du Fu, who spent his teenage in Luoyang, represents the literature of the Heluo region in the Tang Dynasty. At the age of 25, when he traveled to Longmen (called Yique in the ancient times), Henan Province, he wrote the famous poem *Visiting the Fengxian Temple at Longmen Grottoes*.

  A fitful wind blows through gloomy ravines.

  The moon scatters its clear shadows through the branches.

  At such altitude, I am like being close to the stars.

  Just like lying on clouds, I can feel my clothes chill.

  The grandeur of Buddhist temples in the eastern capital was depicted in his poem *Long Men*. The experience that he heard of Li Guinian, a great royal

图5-2　白居易
Figure 5-2　Bai Juyi

musician, singing inspired him to sigh "as blossom falls, so do we meet again!" When he took office in Chang' an (present-day Xi' an), he still came back to Luoyang many times to see his family. It was those times that he created the "Three Officers" and the "Three Partings" achieving realistic poetry at its peak. The culture and life in Luoyang at its heyday made him aspire to start his career in the imperial court with the intention of achieving the Confucian principle of self-cultivating, family-regulating, state-ordering, and world-governing and of cultivating his aesthetic taste of poetry of elegance and orthodoxy.

Poets travelling to Luoyang and living in Luoyang, for example, Li Bai, Meng Haoran, Cen Shen, Meng Jiao, and other poets cannot be neglected given that they all left masterpieces about the beautiful scenery of Luoyang. Li Bai was a great romantic poet. During the years of Tian Bao, he came to Luoyang at times and, for a short time, even lived in seclusion in Songshan Mountain. *Hearing the Sound of Flute in Luoyang in Spring Evening*, *Autumn in Tianjin* and other poems have all become eternal classics. In the third year of Tian Bao (774 AD), Li Bai and Du Fu met in Luoyang. They "were drunk together in the autumn, covered one quilt and then fell asleep, and walked hand in hand with the day" (Du Fu *Seeking for Taoist Fan with Li Bai*). Therefrom, they forged a deep friendship, which became a legend in the history of literature.

In the Song Dynasty, the Heluo region remained a galaxy of literature talents. During the four years when Ouyang Xiu was in Luoyang (West Capital in the Northern Song Dynasty), he tended to write poems together with other poets like Fu Bi.Since then, the famous West Capital Mu-Fu Literati Group was formed and Luoyang became the national center for the creation of poetry and prose and the birthplace of poetry and prose reformation at that time. In "Luoyang Peony", Ouyang Xiu depicted peony characters, explained the connotation of peony names, recorded local customs, and put forward the opinion that "presently, Luoyang' s peony ranks top in the world." He wrote that "Luoyang is a good place to grow flowers, the most outstanding of which is the peony," thereby making Luoyang peony widely known. In Shao Yong' s *Yi Chuan Ji Rang Anthology*, his leisurely and comfortable life characterized by "humming verses at ease, drinking wine delightedly, and being a happy person was reflected." Neo-Confucious poems including *An Impromptu Poem Composed in Spring* and *An Impromptu Poem*

品、释花名、记风俗，认为牡丹"出洛阳者，今为天下第一"。其诗句"洛阳地脉花最重，牡丹尤为天下奇"，使洛阳牡丹家喻户晓。邵雍《伊川击壤集》是他"吟自在诗，饮欢喜酒""为快乐人"的闲适生活之写照。程颢、程颐的理学诗如《春日偶成》《秋日偶成》，颇具思想家兼诗人的伟岸气象。司马光在洛居住长达十五年之久，营建独乐园，编纂了巨著《资治通鉴》。李格非《洛阳名园记》记叙洛阳十七处名园，借诸多名园的兴废盛衰，感叹国家之治乱，得出了"洛阳之盛衰，天下治乱之候也"的结论。

明代河洛小说大家是方汝浩，他著有《禅真逸史》《禅真后史》《东渡记》三部小说，皆假托历史，兼及世情，有着浓重神怪气息，堪称晚明神魔小说的主要代表。清初王铎诗歌展示了明清易代之际的风云变幻以及由明季士大夫到清初贰臣的心路历程，表现出强烈的忧患意识与批判精神。李海观的《歧路灯》为中国古代最为著名的教育小说，被称为"少年之宝筏，为父母者之暮鼓晨钟"。

Composed in Autumn by Cheng Yi and Cheng Hao were about the grandeur of thinkers and poets. Sima Guang lived in Luoyang for as long as fifteen years. In the meantime, he constructed Private Paradise Garden (Du Le Yuan) and wrote the great classic *Comprehensive Mirror to Aid in Government*. Li Gefei described seventeen famed parks in Luoyang in his *Record of Famous Parks* in Luoyang. Through narrating the vicissitude of many popular parks, he lamented the country's failure on governance and concluded that the "ups and downs of Luoyang reflect the state of the country's governance."

Up to the Ming Dynasty (1368 AD-1683 AD), Fang Ruhao was one of the typical novelists in the Heluo region. In his three novels of *The Romance of the Zen*, *The after Romance of the Zen*, and *Damour Journey to the East*, which were rather mythologized and regarded as masterworks of god-evil novels in the late Ming Dynasty, he mirrored the current reality through his description of history. The poetry of Wang Duo, a literati in the early Qing Dynasty (1636 AD-1912 AD), displayed the changeable situation of the transition period between the Ming Dynasty and the Qing Dynasty, and the psychological process of courtiers who were scholar-officials of the Ming Dynasty and were forced to be courtiers of the Qing Dynasty. *A Lantern by the Forked Road* (*Qilu Deng*), written by Li Haiguan, was known as the most famous educational novel in ancient China. It was honored as "the precious raft for young men and epigrams for parents."

二、河洛艺术

河洛地区是中国古代艺术起源的地区。早在距今八九千年的裴李岗文化时期，已经出现了原始音乐和原始美术。文献记载夏王启作"九辩九歌"，孔甲于东阳黄山(今河南偃师首阳山)作《破斧之歌》，为东音之始。商代有"桑林""羽"舞等。周代已经设置专门管理音乐和舞蹈的官职，已有用金(即铜)、石、土、革、丝、木、匏、竹等八种质料制成的各种乐器。

汉代河洛地区书画艺术颇有成就。"熹平石经"是中国历史上最早的官定儒家经典刻石，东汉灵帝熹平四年（175年）至东汉光和六年（183年），蔡邕等人把儒家七经(《鲁诗》《尚书》《周易》《春秋》《公羊传》《仪礼》《论语》)书写并由工匠刻制于46块石碑，竖立于太学门前，"其观视及摹写者，车乘日千余两(辆)，填塞街陌"。蔡邕"篆、隶绝世"，还独创了"飞白体"书法。

图5-3 熹平石经残片

Figure 5-3 Stone Classics of the Xiping Period

II. Art in the Heluo Region

The Heluo region: birthplace of ancient Chinese art

As early as the Peiligang Culture period that can be traced back to eight or nine thousand years ago, there was primitive music and art in this region. According to documentary records, Emperor Qi of the Xia Dynasty (2070 BC-1600 BC) created *Nine Apologies and Nine Songs* (the names of two kinds of ancient songs) while Kong Jia (also the emperor of the Xia Dynasty) produced the song, *The Broken Axe*, in Dongyang's Mount Huang (present-day Mount Shouyang in Yanshi City, Henan Province) then, which was the earliest oriental music. There were also Sang Lin (a kind of dance accompanied by music) and Yu Dance in the Shang Dynasty (1600 BC-1046 BC). By the period of the Zhou Dynasty (1046 BC-256 BC), special official positions were set up to organize musical and dance performances, and people already used eight materials, including metal (bronze), stone, clay, hide, silk, wood, gourd, and bamboo, to manufacture a variety of musical instruments.

In the Han Dynasty (206 BC-220 AD), the Heluo region made significant achievements in terms of calligraphy and painting art. Specifically, the "Stone Classics of the Xiping Period," erected in front of the then Imperial College (in feudal China),was the earliest officially approved stone inscription of Confucian classics in Chinese history. From the fourth year of Xiping (175 AD) to the sixth year of Guanghe (183 AD) of Emperor Ling's reign in the Eastern Han Dynasty (25 AD-220 AD), seven Confucian classics including *The Book of Songs* (the version annotated by Shen Pei of Lu State), *The Book of Documents*, *The Book of Changes*, *The Spring and Autumn Annals*, *The Book Written by Gongyang Gao to Annotate The Spring and Autumn Annals*, *The Book of Ceremonial Etiquette*, and *The Analects of Confucius*, were calligraphed by Cai Yong and other scholars, and later engraved by craftsmen on 46 steles. As described in "The Biography of Cai Yong" in *The Book of the Later Han*, the streets were congested because there were thousands of carriages every day that transported people who wanted to enjoy and copy the stone inscription. What's more, Cai Yong's seal script and clerical script were peerless, at that time, and he also created a style of calligraphy

魏晋南北朝时期河洛艺术多姿多彩。"正始石经"刻于公元241年(三国魏齐王曹芳正始二年),原立于魏都洛阳南郊太学讲堂西侧。因碑文每字皆用古文、小篆和汉隶三种字体写刻,又称"三体石经"。"正始石经"在汉字书法发展史上具有特殊意义,我们从中可以看到汉字书体演变以及多种字体并存的痕迹。钟繇,长期在洛阳为官,他对于已经流行的楷书字体,予以收集、整理、加工,使楷书获得官方认可的地位。魏碑体是一种介于汉晋隶书和唐代楷书之间的新型汉字形体,代表作是"龙门二十品"。其书法方峻严整,结体茂密,点画布满四角,锋芒毕露,十分精美。

隋唐时期洛阳东都歌舞百戏艺术荟萃四方精品,云集八面大家。隋大业六年正月十五日,隋炀帝因为各族酋长来东都朝觐,在洛阳皇城端门南的街道上设置周围五千步的戏场,由天下各地的艺人盛陈百戏,声闻数十里,通宵达旦,灯火通明,一直持续半月之久。吴道子,被奉为"百代画圣",洛阳邙山玄元庙、天宫寺、敬爱寺、福先寺等留有其画作。特别需要说明的是,一代女皇武则天也是书法爱好者,她书写的《升仙太子碑》,以今草为主,辅之以行书,顿挫有力,挥洒自如,整幅作品气韵飘逸,意兴遄飞,直逼书圣王羲之。

唐三彩,是中国古代陶瓷烧制工艺的珍品。它是盛行于唐代的一种低温釉陶器,釉彩有黄、绿、白、褐、蓝、黑等色彩,而以黄、绿、白三色为主,所以人们习惯称之为"唐三彩"。因唐三彩最早、最多出土于洛阳,亦有"洛阳唐三彩"之称。常见的出土唐三彩陶器有三彩马、骆驼、仕女、乐伎俑、枕头等。唐三彩吸纳了中国绘画、雕塑等工艺美术的优点,造型浑厚丰满,工整细腻,线条简朴、流畅,具有独特的艺术风格和鲜明的民族特色。唐三彩不仅在中国的陶瓷史上和美术史上有一定的地位,而且它在中外的文化交流上也起到了重要的促进作用。

宋明清以来河洛艺术不断向民间深入发展。王铎,擅长行书、草书,其《拟山园帖》和《琅华馆帖》最为著名。他的书法作品飞动变

characterized by hollow strokes.

Heluo art was varied and graceful in the Kingdom of Wei (220 AD-265 AD), the Jin Dynasty (265 AD-420 AD), and the Southern and Northern Dynasties (420 AD-589 AD). For instance, the "Stone Classics of Zhengshi Period" was inscribed in the second year of Zhengshi (241 AD) during the reign of Emperor Qi (namely Cao Fang) in the Kingdom of Wei. Originally, it stood in the west of the lecture room of the Imperial College that was located in the southern suburb of Luoyang City, which, at that time, was the capital of Wei. This stone inscription had carvings in three styles of calligraphy, including the classical pre-Qin script, the small seal script, and the clerical script, so it was also called the "Three-script Stone Classics." The Stone Classics of the Zhengshi Period is of special significance in the history of the calligraphy of Chinese characters given that it unveils the evolution of the calligraphic styles of Chinese characters as well as the coexistence of many other fonts from it. Additionally, Zhong Yao, who was an official in Luoyang for a long time has collected, collated, and revised the prevailing regular script at that time transforming it to a standard font that has been recognized by the government. Moreover, the handwriting style of the Wei tablet is a new style of Chinese characters between the Han-Jin dynasties' clerical script and the regular script of the Tang Dynasty (618 AD-907 AD), and it is represented by "The Twenty Select Pieces of Calligraphy of Longmen". With a compact structure, it is square and neat, and its strokes cover the four corners of matts, so it is very exquisite.

During the Sui (581 AD-618 AD) and Tang dynasties, the outstanding acrobatics arts and numerous relevant distinguished performers in the rest of the country all gathered in the Eastern Capital, Luoyang. On the fifteenth day of the first lunar month in the sixth year of Daye in the Sui Dynasty, Emperor Yang established a theatre in the streets in the south of the Imperial City's front gate because the chiefs of some minorities visited Luoyang to have an audience with him. This building was so spacious that to exit the building, people needed to walk about 5,000 steps and it was the venue for artists to perform acrobatics. At that time, people could hear musical sounds even if they were more than ten li (Chinese mile, approximately five hundred meters) away, and the performance lasted through the night. This situation lasted half a month. Moreover, Wu

化,沉雄顿挫,已经达到寓变于毫端、寄情于纸上的超然的艺术境界,有"神笔"之称。河洛地方戏曲品种繁多,其中流传最广的要数河洛大鼓、豫剧等。

图5-4　唐三彩

Figure 5-4　Tri-colored Glazed Pottery of the Tang Dynasty

Daozi was honored as the "Sage of Painting," and there were his drawings in the Xuanyuan Temple, Tiangong Temple, Jing'ai Temple, and Fuxian Temple located on Mangshan Mountain, Luoyang. In particular, Empress Wu Zetian was also a calligraphy lover. *The Stele About the Story of Being Deity of Crown Prince Jin* was mainly written in small cursive script and sometimes in semi-cursive script. It was forceful, free, and full of elegance and charm, and could be on a par with the calligraphy work of Wang Xizhi, the "Sage of Calligraphy."

The tri-colored glazed pottery of the Tang Dynasty is a treasure in the ceramic firing techniques of ancient China and a kind of low-temperature glazed pottery that prevailed in the Tang Dynasty. Although there were yellow, green, white, brown, blue, black, and other glaze colors, yellow, green, and white are mainly used. Consequently, people became used to calling it Tri-colored Glazed Pottery of the Tang Dynasty. Furthermore, this type of pottery was also known as Luoyang Tri-colored Glazed Pottery of the Tang Dynasty because Luoyang City was the earliest and main excavation site. Some common excavated tri-colored glazed pottery of the Tang Dynasty include the tri-colored horse figurine, camel figurine, lady figurine, dancing figurine, and pillow figurine. The strengths of the pottery have been assimilated in Chinese arts and crafts included in traditional painting and sculpture making it vigorous and exquisite in shape and simple and smooth in line that are a display of a unique style and distinctive national characteristics. The tri-colored glazed pottery of the Tang dynasty has not only been of importance in the history of ceramics and arts in China, but it has also greatly promoted cultural exchanges between China and other countries.

Heluo art has further developed by the people in the Song (960 AD-1279 AD), Ming (1368 AD-1644 AD), and Qing (1616 AD-1911 AD) dynasties. For example, Wang Duo was skilled in semi-cursive script and cursive writing and his most famous and well-preserved calligraphy models were *Nishan Models* and *Langhua Models*. His calligraphy works were free and easy with bold and wild brushwork. They have reached the transcendent artistic level, meaning they change strokes and express feelings between the lines. That's why he was known as the "Magic Pen-Wang Duo." Besides, there are a variety of traditional Chinese operas in the Heluo region including Heluo Drum and Henan Opera that were the most widespread.

第六章

播迁交流

Chapter 6

The Spread and Exchange of Heluo Culture

河洛文化作为中国地域文化中的核心文化，具有强大的文化辐射力和影响力。河洛文化对周边区域文化特别是客家文化、闽台文化产生了深远的影响，并跃出国境，传播到东亚、西亚和东南亚国家。

一、河洛郎南迁

史前时代河洛文化已与周边地域文化交流互动。在偃师滑城等地发现的墓葬，不仅随葬有海岱大汶口文化的陶器，还保留有大汶口文化盛行的随葬猪牙和死者拔掉上侧门齿的习俗。此外，长江中游地区的大溪文化、屈家岭文化、石家河文化，长江下游地区的良渚文化，在出土的陶器、玉器中均可见到它们与河洛之间的文化影响。

夏商周时期河洛地区与周边地区的文化交流更加深入。偃师二里头是夏朝国都。后羿是东夷有穷氏之君，乘夏中衰而夺取夏政权。东夷人入主河洛，龙山文化随之涌入河洛。商、周建立后，海岱地区基本上处于它们的统治之下，为河洛地区与齐鲁地区的文化交流提供了便利条件。从江西清江县吴城遗址、湖南全境出土的商代晚期青铜器，从广东清远市出土的商代乐器、兵器等，也可看出这一时期河洛文化对南方地域的广泛影响。

秦汉以来河洛文化对外交流传播的标志性事件，是河洛人数次大规模的南迁，由此形成了客家人和客家文化。客家人是在以河洛人为主体的北方人长期南迁以及迁徙之后再次甚至多次辗转迁徙的过程中形成的。第一次大迁移（317—879年），开始于西晋末年。其时匈奴、鲜卑、羯、氐、羌五个少数民族侵扰以洛阳为中心的中原地区。为逃避战乱，自晋代永嘉以后，中原汉族开始南迁。第二次南迁（公元880年—1126年），开始于唐末至五代时期，安史之乱、黄巢之乱及五代之乱引起迁徙。这次迁徙持续时间较长。第三次迁徙（1127—1644年），开始于宋代。由于金人、元人入侵，部分客家人再度迁徙，先至闽赣的中

As the core part of China's regional cultures, the Heluo culture has had a strong and radiating impact on the cultures of other areas. It has exerted a far-reaching influence on the cultures of peripheral areas especially on the Hakka culture and Min (short for Fujian Province)-Tai (short for Taiwan) culture. It has also spread to other countries in East Asia, West Asia, and Southeast Asia.

Ⅰ. The Migration of Heluo People to the South

The prehistoric age witnessed cultural exchanges between the Heluo region and its neighboring areas. For instance, in cemeteries found in Huacheng Village, Yanshi City, there were burial potteries from Dawenkou Culture in Haidai (Shandong Province) and customs of the Dawenkou period that have prevailed including the manufacture of boar ivory funerary with the dead and extracting the dead's upper incisors. Furthermore, the unearthed potteries and jade wares of Daxi Culture, Qujialing Culture, and Shijiahe Culture in the middle reach of the Yangtze River, as well as Liangzhu Culture in the lower reach of the Yangtze River also illustrate the cultural communication between these areas and the Heluo region.

The cultural exchanges between the Heluo region and its surrounding areas deepened in the Xia, Shang, and Zhou dynasties. Erlitou Village in Yanshi City was the capital of the Xia Dynasty. At one time, Hou Yi, the chieftain of Youqiong Clan Tribe of Dong Yi (the general designation for the eastern nations in ancient China) wrested political power from the Xia Dynasty as it was on its decline. From then, Dong Yi people moved and settled in the Heluo region, bringing with them the Longshan Culture. Since the establishment of the Shang and Zhou dynasties, Haidai area has mainly been under the rule of these two dynasties thereby facilitating cultural exchanges between the Heluo and Qilu regions. Additionally, we can also see the extensive influence of Heluo in Southern China during this period in other objects including unearthed bronzes of the late Shang Dynasty in Wucheng Site, Qingjiang County, Jiangxi Province, and the whole Hunan Province, and musical instruments of the Shang Dynasty as well as weapons excavated from Qingyuan City, Guangdong Province.

Since the Qin (221 BC-206 BC) and Han dynasties, the iconic event that

原氏族再分迁至粤东、粤北。第四次迁徙（1645—1843年），开始于明末清初，因客家内部人口膨胀等原因，第二次、第三次迁移的客家民众再次分头迁徙，一部分"迁至粤之中部及滨海地区，与川桂湘及台湾"。其中四川明末遭张献忠之乱，大量客民移入，即著名的"湖广填四川"。第五次迁徙发生于太平天国起义末期（1866年以后）。客家人分别迁至雷州、钦州、广州、潮汕、香港、澳门等地。这五次迁徙有的是从河洛原居地迁出，有的则是从迁居地往其他地方的二次乃至多次辗转迁徙。客家人就在这漫长的迁徙过程中逐渐形成。

客家人自称为"河洛郎"，他们"根在河洛"。客家人系以汉人为主体，同时包括有"客化"的畲、瑶等少数民族，他们具有共同的利益，具有独特稳定的客家语言、文化、民俗和感情心态（即客家精神）。关于客家人的来源，大量的谱牒、史书等资料证实，客家之源为"中原衣冠旧族"。尽管凡是历史上由山东、山西、河北、陕西及北方其他地区迁居南方，而没与土著居民融合、通婚，并保持汉族血统及文化传统的人都是客家人，但由于河洛区域在历史上所处的特殊地位，在每一次北方人南迁的潮流中，河洛人都占绝大多数，所以"河洛郎"就成为客家人的称谓，也即客家人、客家文化"根在河洛"。

闽台文化的形成可源溯于河洛文化。宋代程颢程颐创立的洛学，在福建传播，主要是通过福建籍程门弟子杨时、游酢、罗从彦进行，经过李侗、朱熹的继承和阐发，形成了闽学思想文化体系。朱熹是闽学集大成者，又是二程洛学的发扬光大者，后人将他的学说和二程的学说联系起来，称为"程朱理学"。泉州是闽南文化的代表地区，长期以来其敬重儒学之风颇盛，而追本溯源在于深受河洛文化传统的影响。

台湾文化的建构成分是河洛文化、客家文化、闽南文化，在长期的历史演变过程中形成台湾乡土文化，是中华文化的延伸和发展。台湾人的构成主体是闽南人、客家人，其所讲的闽南话，源自魏晋南北朝河洛地区的雅音，因而又称"河洛话"。研究分析台湾民俗，其节日、婚

marked exchanges with foreigners and the spread of Heluo culture was the mass migration of Heluo people to the South, a process which involved Hakka people and their culture. At that time, Northerners, who were mainly composed of Heluo men, migrated to the South over a long time, then moved again or even repeatedly after this migration. During the process of mass migrations, Hakka people came into being. The first mass migration (317 AD-879 AD) occurred in the late Western Jin Dynasty (265 AD-317 AD) when five ethnic minorities in ancient China, including Xiongnu, Xianbei, Jie, Di, and Qiang intruded into the Luoyang-centered Central Plains. From the Yongjia period of the Western Jin Dynasty, ongoing disruptive wars forced the Han nation in the Central Plains to migrate southward. The second migration to the South (880 AD-1126 AD), which lasted for a long time, happened from the Tang Dynasty to the Five Dynasties (907 AD-960 AD) because of An Lushan Rebellion (755 AD-763 AD), Huang Chao Uprising (875 AD-884 AD), and Chaos in the Five Dynasties. The third migration (from 1127 AD to 1644 AD) took place in the Song Dynasty. Some Hakka people moved again because of the invasion of the Jin State (1115 AD-1234 AD) and the Yuan Dynasty (1206 AD-1368 AD) while some of the migrants who arrived in Fujian and Jiangxi Provinces were later again forced to remigrate to eastern and northern Guangdong (short for Yue). In the late Ming and early Qing dynasties, the fourth migration (1645 AD-1843 AD) happened. At that time, an explosion of the Hakka population and other factors meant some Hakka people who had moved in the second and third migrations "have remigrated to the central area and coastal region of Guangdong, Sichuan (short for Chuan), Guangxi (short for Gui), Hunan (short for Xiang) and Taiwan." Because of the movement, Zhang Xianzhong started a massacre in Sichuan Province in the late Ming Dynasty resulting in a sharp decrease in the local population and triggering the arrival of immigrants. This was the famous "Hunan, Hubei, and Guangdong people's Migration to Sichuan Province." Finally, the fifth migration (after 1866 AD) occurred in the late stage of the Taiping Rebellion (the largest peasant uprising in Chinese history) when Hakka people migrated to Leizhou City, Guangzhou City, and Chaoshan area in Guangdong, Qinzhou City in Guangxi, Hong Kong, Macao, and other areas respectively. During the process of these five migrations, some people directly moved out from their hometowns

图6-1 洛阳出土的东汉墓玻璃瓶

Figure 6-1 Glass Bottle of Eastern Han Dynasty, unearthed in Luoyang

in the Heluo region while others re-migrated to other areas from their residence through secondary or even multiple migrations. Gradually, Hakka people came into being during the lengthy process of migration.

Hakka people claim to be "Heluo Fellows" and always remember their "Roots Are in Heluo." Hakka (the sub-nation of the Han nationality) mainly includes Han people and some ethnic minorities including the She and Yao nationalities that are influenced by Hakka culture. They have shared interests, and the unique and stable Hakka dialect, culture, folklore, and mentality (Hakka spirit). As to the origin of Hakka people, a lot of family trees, historical records, and other materials have confirmed that they came from "the once rich and powerful families in the Central Plains." Hakka People also include those who have migrated to the South from Shandong, Shanxi, Hebei, Shaanxi Provinces, and other northern areas in Chinese history, but haven't intermarried with local people and have remained descendants of Han nationality and its cultural traditions. Even so, because the Heluo region has played a special role in history and its people were the overwhelming majority during each migration from the north to the south, Hakka people have been called "Heluo Fellows," that is, Hakka people and their cultural are "rooted in Heluo."

The formation of Min-Tai culture can be traced back to Heluo culture. The Learning of Luo founded by Cheng Hao (1032 AD-1085 AD) and Cheng Yi (1033 AD-1107 AD) of the Northern Song Dynasty (960 AD-1127 AD) was disseminated in Fujian by their Fujian disciples, Yang Shi, You Zuo, and Luo Congyan, then inherited and elucidated by Li Dong and Zhu Xi of the Southern Song Dynasty (1127 AD-1279 AD). Finally, the ideological and cultural system of the Min School has formed. Zhu Xi not only epitomized the Min School but also carried forward the Learning of Luo initiated by the Cheng Brothers. Consequently, later generations combined the Cheng Brothers and Zhu theories and called this "Cheng-Zhu Neo-Confucianism." Quanzhou City in Fujian is the representative area of Minnan (Southern Fujian) culture. The habit of deeply respecting Confucianism flourished there for some time because it was profoundly influenced by the cultural tradition of the Heluo region.

嫁、丧葬、祭祀等，大多源于河洛古风。

　　河洛郎虽屡次迁徙，但有着强烈的返本追祖意识。他们为了减轻心中的思乡之痛，把河洛的地名带到了移入地区，以北方故地之名命新驻地之名。如到闽南的中原人把所在地的两条河分别起名为"晋江"和"洛阳江"，称洛阳江上所修建之桥为"洛阳桥"。客家人的家谱详述家族源流，对自我的起源地河洛地区更是有着难以割舍的情怀，在家谱中每每述及。客家人对河洛或中原先祖的语言、风俗、精神品质都有着强烈的固守与传承。

The components of Taiwan culture include Heluo culture, Hakka culture, and Minnan culture. Their development to become the local culture of Taiwan is of long-standing historical evolution which is also the extension and development of the Chinese culture. In addition, Taiwan people are mainly comprised of Minnan and Hakka people, and the Minnan dialect they speak nowadays originated from the standard language of the Heluo region in Wei, Jin, and Southern and Northern dynasties. Therefore, it is also called the "Heluo accent." Research and analysis indicate that Taiwan's folklore including festivals, marriages, funerals, and sacrifices were largely derived from the ancient customs in the Heluo region.

Although "Heluo Fellows" migrated to other places multiple times, they continued to maintain a strong root-seeking consciousness. In order to alleviate their homesickness, Heluo people brought the geographical names of the Heluo region to places to which they migrated. In other words, they named their new places of residence after the name of their hometowns in the North. For example, people in the Central Plains who migrated to Southern Fujian called two local rivers "Jin River" and "Luoyang River" respectively, and referred to the bridge built over the Luoyang River as "Luoyang Bridge." Additionally, Hakka people have elaborated on the origins and development of their family trees. In particular, they were filled with nostalgia for their ancestral home, the Heluo region, so they mentioned it in their family trees. Finally, Hakka people also stuck to and inherited the language, customs, and spiritual character from their ancestors in the Heluo region or the Central Plains.

二、向东亚播迁

朝鲜半岛与河洛地区的文化交流可以上溯到商王朝时期。汉初伏生的《尚书大传·洪范》有"箕子朝鲜"的记载。尽管尚有争论,大多认为箕子东走朝鲜,将河洛地区已经成熟的文化典籍传播到这一地区,使这里的民众受到河洛文化的浸染。曹魏、西晋、北魏时期,朝鲜半岛的政权多次派遣使者来帝都洛阳朝贡,朝廷派遣使者回访,两国间的政治、文化来往增多。

隋代与朝鲜半岛的高丽、百济、新罗三国交往与日俱增。隋文帝所定的《七部乐》中即有一部为《高丽伎》。高丽效法河洛地区的都城建设形制,其首都平壤城"东西六里",与汉魏洛阳城的"九六"之制相合。河洛地区封建王朝的校猎之制、赋税制度也被高丽所吸收。朝鲜半岛"居父母及夫之丧,服皆三年"的服丧制度,也借鉴了河洛地区封建王朝的定制。这一时期朝鲜半岛推行汉字,大量的儒家经典为其所喜爱。

唐代以河洛地区为代表的唐文化对朝鲜半岛的礼乐制度、社会风俗、文化教育和宗教都产生了广泛而持久的影响。唐武后垂拱二年(686年),新罗派遣使者来洛阳朝贡,"因上表请《唐礼》一部并杂文章,则天令所司写《吉凶要礼》,并于《文馆词林》采其词涉规诫者,勒成五十卷以赐之"。高丽的乐舞引起武则天时代士大夫的喜爱,神都朝堂之上甚至有人能够舞蹈之。从洛阳邙山发现的黑齿常之父子等朝鲜人的墓葬,也可说明洛阳与朝鲜半岛之间交往的深远。

中日两国是一衣带水的邻邦,河洛地区作为自先秦以来中华民族文化的核心地带,在与日本列岛的交往过程中发挥着重要的作用。东汉时期日本使节曾两次来洛阳朝贡。第一次在建武中元二年(57年),"倭奴国奉贡朝贺,使人自称大夫,倭国之极南界也。光武赐以印绶"。这

II. The Spread of Heluo Culture to East Asia

The cultural exchanges between the Korean Peninsula and Heluo region can be traced back as early as to the Shang Dynasty. In *The Explanatory Work About the Book of Documents*, an article entitled Hongfan (nine ways of governing a country proposed by Jizi, the nobility of the late Shang Dynasty, to Emperor Wu in the Zhou Dynasty) written by Fu Sheng of the early Han Dynasty, had an account of "Gija (the Korean pronunciation of Jizi) Joseon" (the regime established in the north of the Korean Peninsula by Jizi). Although it was controversial, most of the people thought that Jizi went east to North Korea, and spread the outstanding cultural books and records of the Heluo region there, thus spreading Heluo culture and deepening its influence among the local people. During the period of the Kingdom of Wei, Western Jin, and Northern Wei (386 AD-534 AD) dynasties, the Korean Peninsula's regimes frequently dispatched envoys to the Imperial Capital, Luoyang, to pay tribute, while the imperial courts equally sent out ambassadors to pay return visits. As a result, the political and cultural exchanges between China and North Korea increased day by day.

The Sui Dynasty's contact with three states on the Korean Peninsula, including Koryo, Paekche, and Silla, grew with each passing day. For example, the court music in the reign of Emperor Wen of the Sui Dynasty was categorized into seven types and one of them was Koryo Music. Additionally, the Koryo State imitated the shape and structure of the capital of the Heluo region. Its capital, Pyongyang City, was "six li long from east to west," while the Han-Wei Ancient City of Luoyang was "nine li in length (from north to south) and six li in width (from east to west)." In the meantime, the system of hunting and taxes of feudal dynasties in the Heluo region were assimilated by Koryo. Moreover, in the Korean Peninsula, "if parents or husbands passed away, their kids or wives had to mourn for three years." Reference to this system of mourning has been made to the feudal dynasties in the Heluo area. During this period, the Korean Peninsula popularized Chinese characters so that a considerable number of Confucian classics are significanly loved in the peninsula.

The Tang culture represented by the Heluo region widely and enduringly

里提到了倭国使节自称"大夫",而大夫这一词完全来自河洛地区已经成熟的称谓。光武帝所赐的印绶在1784年被福冈市志贺岛的一位农民发现,"汉倭奴国王"字样历经千年依旧清晰。

第二次是在汉安帝永初元年,"倭国王师升等遣使奉献口百六十,愿请见"。魏晋时期,东瀛岛国势力最强者为邪马台国,控驭藩属二十余国,三次来洛阳朝贡,中国朝廷赠予日方大量礼品,河洛地区成熟的纺织技术、冶铁技术可能随之传到了日本。

隋唐时期以遣隋使和遣唐使为代表的中日文化交流达到鼎盛。隋朝时期,日本派遣使者来中国朝贡,共计四次,以洛阳为终点的三次。唐朝日本共计派遣十九次遣唐使,成行者十五次,其中高宗显庆四年(659年)、麟德二年(665年)、武后长安二年(702年)是以洛阳为终点,而开元五年(717年)、开元二十一年(733年)玄宗在洛阳接见了遣唐使者。这些使者来华,同行者还有留学生、留学僧,使日本开始了全面学习隋唐文化的时代。他们将学习带回去的隋唐制度如均田制、租庸调制、僧侣制度,移植成为日本的重要制度。在国家政治体制借鉴方面,日本确立了以天皇为中心的政治体制,颁行了"制七色一十三阶之冠"的冠位制度,地方国、郡、里的官僚机构设置也沿袭了隋唐的制度。受武则天造大佛铜像、通天浮屠以及在龙门奉先寺雕刻卢舍那大佛石像的启发,日本圣武天皇于奈良以东(现东大寺的位置)建起以洛阳龙门石窟卢舍那大佛坐像为原型的高达14.9米的大佛坐像,该佛像也称奈良大佛。另外,唐三彩产品在日本的福冈、奈良等许多地方不断出土,均为巩义窑的制品。日本汉诗中也有大量的"洛阳"意象与书写,无论是实际语义、借用典故还是使用氛围,都与中国传统文学形象中的洛阳一脉相承。

综观日本所派遣的遣隋使、遣唐使,数次以洛阳为终点,在洛阳朝见隋唐皇帝,表明洛阳在中日文化交流中具有重要的地位,他们作为中日文化交流的信使,将植根于河洛大地的中华民族优秀文化传播到遥远

influenced the Korean Peninsula's system of rites and music, social customs, cultural education, and religion during the Tang Dynasty. In the second year of Chuigong(686 AD) of Empress Wu Zetian's reign during the Tang Dynasty, Silla dispatched envoys to Luoyang to pay tribute. At that time "these envoys have presented a memorial to the empress to ask for *The Rites of Tang* and other articles, so Wu Zetian has ordered the department concerned to write *The Crucial Rites About Good or Ill Luck* and to extract some statements about admonishment from *Wen Guan Ci Lin* (a collection of poems and essays from the Han Dynasty to Emperor Taizong's reign during the Tang Dynasty), which were finally compiled into 50 volumes to give them." Meanwhile, Koryo's dance accompanied by music enjoyed great popularity among the scholar-officials during Empress Wu's reign and people in the imperial court of the "Divine Capital" could even perform it. Moreover, the cemeteries of Heukchi Sangji and his son, as well as other Koreans found in Mangshan Mountain, also showed the profound and lasting communication between Luoyang and the Korean Peninsula.

China and Japan are close neighbors separated only by a narrow strip of water. As the core zone of the Chinese culture since the pre-Qin period (namely before 221 BC), the Heluo region has played an important part in China's contact with the Japanese Archipelago. In the Eastern Han Dynasty, Japanese envoys went to Luoyang twice to present tribute. To be specific, the first visit took place in the second year of Zhongyuan (57 AD)during the reign of Emperor Guangwu. At that time, "these envoys have paid tribute to the imperial court to show respect. They even called themselves 'Dafu' (a senior official title in feudal China) and said that their country lies in the southernmost part of Japan. Therefore, the emperor has awarded them an official seal with a silk ribbon." In the above-mentioned event, Japanese envoys called themselves "Dafu," but it was a mature appellation used at that time in the Heluo region. Moreover, the official seal with a silk ribbon awarded by Emperor Guangwu has been found by a farmer in Shikanoshima, Fukuoka, Japan. Although more than one thousand years have passed, the Chinese characters on it, literally, King of the dependency of Japan are still clearly visible.

The second visit happened in the first year of the Yongchu period of Emperor An. According to historical documents, "Shi Sheng and other Japanese emperors

图6-2 日本遣唐使
Figure 6-2 Japanese Missions to China in the Tang Dynasty

have dispatched envoys to present 160 slaves to the Eastern Han Dynasty and request an interview with its emperor." In the Wei and Jin dynasties, Yamataikoku, then the most powerful realm in Japan, possessed more than twenty vassal states and went to Luoyang to pay tribute three times, while the imperial court gave a lot of gifts to Japan. Therefore, the mature textile and iron-smelting technologies in the Heluo region were probably taken to Japan as part of these gifts.

In the Sui and Tang dynasties, Sino-Japan cultural exchanges represented by Japanese diplomats dispatched to the Sui and Tang dynasties reached their peak. During the Sui Dynasty, Japan sent out envoys to China to present tribute four times, and three of these visits were to Luoyang. Furthermore, Japan dispatched 19 groups of emissaries to the Tang Dynasty, and 15 of them finally arrived in China. 3 groups set feet in Luoyang in the fourth year of Xianqing (659 AD), the second year of Linde (665 AD) during the reign of Emperor Gao Zong, and the second year of Chang'an(702 AD) during Empress Wu's reign respectively. In the fifth year(717 AD) and the twenty-first year (733 AD) of Kaiyuan, Emperor Xuan Zong met with the Japanese emissaries in Luoyang. The envoys have come to China with Japanese students and monks. Since then, Japan began to comprehensively study the culture of the Sui-Tang dynasties. These two dynasty systems that they learned and brought to Japan including the system of land equalization, the Zu-yong-diao System (a type of head tax system),and the monastic management system have all developed into crucial Japanese systems. In terms of using China's political systems for reference, Japan has established the tenno-centered political system. It issued and implemented the crown-office system that includes crowns in seven different colors indicating thirteen grades of official ranks. Its three-level administrative structure—Koku, Gun, and Ri, followed the systems of the Sui and Tang dynasties.Enlightened by the giant bronze Buddha statue, the sky-high Buddhist stupa, and the grand stone statue of Vairocana Buddha in the Fengxian Temple of Longmen Grottoes in the period of Empress Wu Zetian of the Tang Dynasty, Japan's Tenno Shomu gave an order to build a giant sitting Buddha statue in the east of Nara (present-day Todai-ji) and it was also called the Giant Bronze Buddha in Nara. This 14.9-meter high Buddha statue took the giant sitting Buddha statue of Vairocana in Luoyang's Longmen Grottoes as the prototype. Moreover, the tri-colored potteries of the

图6-3 洛阳龙门（局部）
Figure 6-3 Longmen Grottoes (Part)

Tang Dynasty have constantly been unearthed in Fukuoka, Nara, and many other places in Japan, and they were all fired in the Kiln of Gong County in Henan Province. Meanwhile, there are a lot of images and descriptions about Luoyang in Japan's Chinese poetry. These images and descriptions are quite similar to Luoyang in traditional Chinese literature in terms of semantic meaning, allusions elicited and occasions for use.

Throughout history, the Japanese envoys to the Sui and Tang dynasties have, on many occasions, made Luoyang their destination and had audiences with emperors of the Sui-Tang dynasties, which shows the critical role that Luoyang has played in Sino-Japan cultural exchanges. As the messengers of cultural communication between China and Japan, they have spread the Chinese nation's outstanding cultures that are rooted in the Heluo region in Japan where they continue to significantly contribute to fostering Heluo culture.

Japan's urban construction has been deeply influenced by Luoyang City of the Sui and Tang dynasties. For instance, Fujiwara-kyō that was built in the seventh century was an imitation of Luoyang City of the Sui-Tang dynasties in its shape and structure. Additionally, Kyoto's buildings and other capitals in Japan all originated from Chang'an and Luoyang in the Tang Dynasty. According to *The Emperor Annals*, during Tenno Kammu's reign in Japan, "Sakyo Ku built in the east of Kyoto at that was an imitation of Luoyang City in the Tang Dynasty in terms of the architecture." For example, the names of Tongtuo Fang (Fang refers to the residential area of the Tang Dynasty), Jiaoye Fang, Xuanfeng Fang, Chunfeng Fang, Anzhong Fang, Taohua Fang, Fengcai Fang, and Yucai Fang in Sakyo Ku were borrowed from Luoyang City. Apart from Yingtian Gate, the names of Shangdong Gate and Shangxi Gate of the Palace City also imitated those in Luoyang City during the Han-Wei Dynasties. Consequently, the Japanese habitually called Kyoto "Kyoraku." This appellation is still used today and a series of new derivative words including Jyouraku, Rakuchuu, and Rakugai have been formed.

The cultural exchanges between China and Japan had begun to decline in the Song Dynasty, although such a decline was not perceptible. On the contrary, exchanges continued to exist in other ways. In March in the ninth year of Emperor Tai Zong's reign, monks from Todai-ji in Nara, Japan, presented to the

的日本，对于河洛文化的发扬光大起了有力的促进作用。

日本城市建设也深受隋唐洛阳城的影响。兴建于7世纪的日本藤原京，在都城形制上模仿隋唐洛阳城。日本京都的宫室、都城的源流都出自唐代的长安城和洛阳城，《帝王编年纪》记载，恒武天皇时"东京左京，唐名洛阳"。左京中的铜驼、教业、宣风、淳风、安众、陶化、丰财、毓财等8个坊名仿自洛阳，除了应天门以外，宫城的上东门、上西门之名也仿自汉魏时期的洛阳城。将京都称为"京洛"，已成为日本人的习惯，这个称呼沿用至今，并衍生出"上洛""洛中""洛外"等一系列新的词语。

虽然中日文化交流在宋代开始趋于衰落，但并没有由此沉落，而是以其他方式继续存在。宋太宗太平兴国九年三月，日本奈良东大寺僧人朝贡，在洛阳朝见了宋太宗，献铜器十余事，并日本《职员》《年代纪》各一卷。宋太宗召见他们后，存拊甚厚，赐紫衣，给郑氏注《孝经》一卷、记室参军任希古撰《越王孝经新义》一卷，印本《大藏经》一部。这件事情说明中日之间的往来并没有随着历史的推移而中断。

imperial court their tribute which included more than ten kinds of bronze wares and Japanese books like *Zhiyuan* and *The Chronicle*, and had an audience with the emperor in Luoyang. After meeting them, Emperor Tai Zong gave them numerous utensils, purple royal robes (uniforms that senior officials of the Song Dynasty wore), a volume of *The Classic of Filial Piety* annotated by Zheng Xuan, a volume of *The New Explanations About the Classic of Filial Piety of King Gou Jian of Yue* written by Ren Xigu, and a printed copy of *Tripitaka*. Through this event, we can see that, in reality, the Sino-Japan exchanges were not interrupted as time went on.

三、沿丝绸之路西传

东汉以降,西域各国经过丝绸之路到洛阳朝贡、贸易和传教。在此过程中,河洛文化以海纳百川的气度吸收外来文化的营养,并推动了河洛文化的对外传播与交流。

东汉到北魏时期河洛文化沿丝绸之路对外传播与交流,有西行与东来的区别。在洛阳登坛受戒的僧人朱士行西度流沙,到达于阗(今新疆和田),得《大品般若经》梵本,遣弟子送还洛阳,译为《放光般若经》。北魏神龟元年(518年),宋云与比丘惠生,受胡太后之诏,出使西域,由京城洛阳出发,于十二月初进入乌场国(在古北印度一带),寻访佛祖坐处、晒袈裟处、"投身饲饿虎之处"、"剥皮为纸,折骨为笔"处等胜迹,于正光三年(522年)回到洛阳,取回大乘经典一百七十部,丰富了中国的佛教文化。在从洛阳出发西行的同时,还有西域众多国家地区沿丝绸之路东来,到洛阳帝都"东向而朝天子""献方奇""纳爱质",以及从事其他商贸、文化、宗教活动。各国的使节、商贾、僧侣给洛阳的文化、艺术、宗教乃至日常生活带来巨大影响,胡风骤起,尤以灵帝时期为甚,好胡服、胡帐、胡床、胡坐、胡饭、胡箜篌、胡笛、胡舞,京师贵戚竟为之。《后汉书·西域传》《晋书·四夷传》等在介绍西域诸国时,凡记载距离里程的,皆以洛阳为起点,如《域传》记疏勒国"去洛阳万三百里"、安息国"去洛阳二万五千里"等,这从一个侧面表明洛阳城是名副其实的丝绸之路的东方起点。

隋唐时期的洛阳城,是驰名世界的国际大都会。尤其是大运河的通航,更使洛阳成为全国水陆交通的中心、经济商贸的中心以及国际交往的中心。除了著名的玄奘"西天取经",还有另一位赴"西天取经"的高僧义净。据《大唐西域求法高僧传》记载:义净经海路,于咸亨四年

III. The Spread of Heluo Culture to the Western Regions Along the Silk Road

After the Eastern Han Dynasty, western countries came to Luoyang via the Silk Road to pay tribute, trade, and do missionary work. During this process, Heluo culture absorbed the quintessence of foreign culture in a spirit of inclusiveness that facilitated its external spread and dissemination.

From the Eastern Han Dynasty to the Northern Wei Dynasty, Heluo culture spread to other countries and was sustained by way of cultural exchanges along the Silk Road. During this process, Chinese people went west while foreigners came east. Zhu Shixing, a monk who had once boarded the precept platform and received commandments in Luoyang, traveled westward over quicksand and ultimately arrived at Khotan (present-day Hotan City in Xinjiang). He has obtained the *Mahaprajnaparama Sutra* written in Sanskrit and let his disciples deliver it at Luoyang where it was later translated into (*Fang Guang Bo Re Jing* (the name of a Chinese Buddhist Scripture). In the first year of Shengui (518 AD) of the Northern Wei Dynasty, instructed by Queen Mother Hu, Song Yun, and Hui Sheng (a Buddhist monk) went to the Western Regions. These two people departed from the capital Luoyang and arrived in Uddiyana (in ancient Northern India) in early December. They sought and visited in famous historical sites including places where Buddhas sat in meditation, where they hung out their kasaya, where they sacrificed themselves to feed hungry tigers, and where they peeled off their skin and used it as paper and broke their bones which served as pens to write the Buddhist verse. Finally, in the third year of Zhengguang (522 AD), Song Yun and Hui Sheng returned to Luoyang with 170 Mahayana Buddhism's sutras that immensely enriched China's Buddhist culture. When Chinese people went westward from Luoyang, many people in western countries and regions also went eastward along the Silk Road to Luoyang. These people "have paid respects to the emperor eastward, and presented the imperial court with exotic goods produced everywhere and hostages." Furthermore, they have also engaged in other commercial trade as well as cultural and religious activities. Envoys, merchants, and monks from various countries have exerted

到达耽摩立底国（今孟加拉国等地）与中天竺。曾先后遍游鹫峰、鸡足山、鹿野苑、祇林精舍等佛教圣地，在那烂陀寺学习佛法。前后经25年，历30多个国家，于武周证圣元年（695）仲夏返达神都洛阳，武则天亲迎于上东门。王玄策，唐洛州洛阳人，曾先后三次以大唐官方使节的身份出使印度，并把从印度取回的弥勒菩萨新样供奉在洛阳敬爱寺中。

在官、私、僧、俗沿丝绸之路西行的同时，也有众多的西域使者、商人、僧人沿丝绸之路东来，其中东抵洛阳者为数甚多。大业十一年（615年）正月，隋炀帝在洛阳举行盛大宴会，西域诸国遣使朝贡，当时为了安置这些远道而来的西域人，隋炀帝特在洛阳置四方馆。《旧唐书·西戎传》记载了拂菻国（东罗马帝国）遣使来华、来洛的具体情况。号称"开元三大士"的善无畏、金刚智、不空，均沿丝绸之路来华，是中国佛教密宗的创立者，他们都曾在洛阳传教说法。洛阳也有一定数量的景教、祆教、摩尼教僧侣。如唐后期洛阳大秦寺的寺主是法和玄应，僧侣有大德玄庆、志通，他们是来自中亚信仰景教的粟特人。洛阳地区唐墓出土了大量胡人俑，有武官俑、乐舞俑、牵马牵驼俑以及身背行囊的胡商俑、胡侍俑，这是当年洛阳城各色外来移民的形象写照。

东西方的经济文化交流丰富了河洛地区的物质与文化生活。在河洛地区日常生活中，流行于东罗马拜占庭时期的高足杯、流行于波斯萨珊时期的多曲长杯等大量外来器物被使用。从洛阳墓葬出土的双鱼纹四曲金长杯、三彩凤首壶、兽首壶，其造型和装饰源于波斯萨珊王朝时期的胡瓶，说明其在当时洛阳官僚贵族生活中使用非常普遍。洛阳流行胡乐，据《羯鼓录》记载，名相宋璟的女儿经常在洛阳宅第中练习羯鼓。神龙元年（705年）十一月，唐中宗在洛阳城南门楼观看泼寒胡戏。起源于波斯的马球体育运动也传入河洛地区，河南府告成县百姓王利文宅北坂之下辟有球场，唐玄宗身为亲王时，"自夏徂秋，往来游赏"。后唐庄宗多次和王公大臣在洛阳鞠场击球。在外来马球的基础上，河洛地

considerable influence on Luoyang culture, art, religion, and even the daily life of its people. At that time, objects introduced from the northern and western nationalities of China or from abroad (the term used to describe these places is Hu) suddenly prevailed in Luoyang, especially during the reign of Emperor Ling of the Eastern Han Dynasty. He was very fond of the Hu costume, Hu tent, Hu bed, Hu people's sitting position, Hu rice, Hu Konghou (an ancient plucked stringed instrument), Hu flute and Hu dance, and the nobility in the capital all competitively imitated him. In a volume entitled *The Biography of the Western Regions* in *The Book of the Later Han*, *The Biography of Four Clan Tribes* in *The Book of the Jin Dynasty*, and other historical books, the introduction of western countries, whenever it was based on distance, took Luoyang as the starting point. For example, as noted in *The Biography of the Western Regions*, Shu-lig is ten thousand and three hundred li away from Luoyang, and there is twenty-five thousand li between Parthia Empire and Luoyang. This shows that Luoyang City is the genuine eastern starting point of the Silk Road at that time.

During the Sui and Tang dynasties, Luoyang was a world-renowned international metropolis. It is worth mentioning that Luoyang became the hub of land and water transportation, the economic and commercial center, and the center of international communication throughout the country since the opening of the Grand Canal during this period. Apart from Xuanzang who went to India to bring Buddhist scriptures to China, another eminent monk from Luoyang, Yi Jing, also went to India for Buddhist Sutras. According to *The Biography of Eminent Monks Striven for Buddhist Scriptures in the Western Regions* in the Tang Dynasty, Yijing finally arrived in Tamralipti (present-day Bangladesh and other regions) and Central Tianzhu (ancient India) by sea in the fourth year of Xianheng of the Tang Dynasty. He traveled to Jiu Summit, Mount Jizu, Sarnath, Zhilin Vihara, and other Buddhist holy lands consecutively, and studied Buddha dharma in India's Nalanda Monastery. The trip covered over 30 countries spanning 25 years before Yijing returned to the Divine Capital Luoyang in the midsummer of the first year of Zhengsheng (695 AD) of the Wu-Zhou Dynasty (690 AD-705 AD). At that time, even Empress Wu Zetian personally greeted him at Shangdong Gate. Additionally, Wang Xuance, a Luoyang native in the Tang Dynasty, went on a diplomatic mission to India as the official envoy of the

图6-4 玄奘西行
Figure 6-4 Xuan Zang going West

Tang Dynasty three times during which he brought back the newly-designed bodhisattva Maitreya that was consecrated in Jing'ai Temple in Luoyang.

When officials, individuals, monks, and common people in China went westwards along the Silk Road, many envoys, merchants, monks of the Western Regions came along this route. Among these journeys, the number of people that reached Luoyang finally was large. In the lunar January of the eleventh year of Daye (615 AD), Emperor Yang of the Sui Dynasty held grand banquets in Luoyang and western countries all sent envoys to pay tribute to the imperial court. A special order was given to He to build a mansion named Sifang in Luoyang to serve as accommodation for distinguished Westerners coming from afar. In *The Old Book of Tang*, a volume entitled *The Biography of Xi Rong Tribe* recorded the specific circumstance when the Byzantine Empire (namely the Eastern Roman Empire, 395 AD-1453 AD) dispatched ambassadors to China and even Luoyang. Three Indian eminent monks, Subhakarasimha, Vajrabodhi, and Amoghavajra, known as the "Three Grand Masters of the Kaiyuan Period," also came to China along the Silk Road. They created Chinese Buddhism, also known as Esoteric Buddhism, and preached Buddhism and Dharma in Luoyang. In addition, there were a certain number of monks and priests from Nestorianism, Zoroastrianism, and Manicheism in Luoyang. For example, during the later Tang Dynasty, the head monk of Da Qin Temple in Luoyang was Fahe Xuanying and there were also other monks like Bhadanta Xuanqing and Zhitong. They were all Sogdians who believed in Nestorianism in Central Asia. Moreover, a large number of figurines of the Hu people (minorities from northern and western China, or foreigners) were excavated from the tombs of the Tang Dynasty in Luoyang, including figurines of military officers, figurines of dancers, figurines of Hu people walking with (a) horse(s) or camel(s), figurines of Hu merchants carrying traveling bags, and figurines of Hu imperial bodyguards that were all a vivid portrayal of various migrants in Luoyang City in those years.

Economic and cultural exchanges between the East and the West enriched the material and cultural life of Heluo people. In the daily life of Heluo men, the stem cups that prevailed during the period of the Byzantine Empire, the oblong cups in the period of Sassanian Persia (226 AD-651 AD), and other foreign utensils were frequently used. The modeling and ornamentation of gold oblong

区在唐代还出现了骑驴击球。

　　河洛地区与东南亚的交往是与南越地区渐次开发联系在一起的。汉魏时期，东南亚地区的国家多次派遣使节辗转到达洛阳进行朝贡。东汉建武十三年（37年）九月，"日南徼外蛮夷（柬埔寨）献白雉、白兔"，这是《后汉书》记载的最早遣使访华的东南亚国家。叶调（今印度尼西亚爪哇岛或苏门答腊岛）、敦忍乙（今缅甸），也先后遣使来到东汉帝都洛阳。隋朝与东南亚地区见诸记载交往的仅有四国，分别为林邑（今越南中部）、赤土（学者大多主张在今马来西亚北部一带）、真腊（今柬埔寨）、婆利国（或以为在今印度尼西亚加里曼丹岛，或以为在今印度尼西亚巴厘岛）。唐代以降，不少河洛地区的诗人如杜审言、沈佺期、刘禹锡等人都先后到达过安南（今越南），并留下了许多诗文。

　　河洛文化自形成以来在海内外广泛传播与交流。国内从黄河流域到长江流域，河洛文化不断南迁且与当地文化融合，逐渐形成了与其"同根同源"的客家文化、闽南文化、台湾文化，并通过它们向东南亚扩散发展。河洛文化向东传播，从先秦两汉的经济往来，到魏晋时期的政治体制效仿，再到隋唐时期直接派遣留学生，都证明了对朝鲜半岛和日本列岛文化影响的日益深远。河洛文化从丝绸之路的东方起点洛阳向西域、中亚、西亚、欧洲传播，汉魏与隋唐的洛阳帝都见证了这一时期文化交流的盛况。

　　河洛文化在当代已成为对外文化交流的一张名片。1989年至今，已先后举办了十五届河洛文化国际学术研讨会，从以洛阳为中心的研讨活动，发展到以河南为中心，再到广东、台湾、江西、福建等地，来自海峡两岸、港澳地区以及日本、韩国、新加坡、马来西亚、美国、英国、德国、俄罗斯、越南、泰国、澳大利亚、新西兰、菲律宾、意大利、奥地利、比利时、巴西、阿根廷等国的专家学者积极参会并热烈地进行对话与交流，《人民日报》（海外版）、《华声报》、美国《星岛日报》等新闻媒体对研讨会的盛况相继进行了报道，这使河洛文化成为中华文

cups with double fish, pots with tricolored phoenixes' heads, and pots with beasts' heads unearthed from the tombs in Luoyang all originated from the Hu bottles of Sassanian Persia, an indication that they were widely used by bureaucrats and the nobility in Luoyang.Hu music was once popular in Luoyang. According to *The Record of Jie Drum*, the daughter of Song Jing, the well-known prime minister during the Tang Dynasty, often practiced Jie drum in her mansion in Luoyang. In November of the first year of Shenlong (705 AD), Emperor Zhong Zong of the Tang Dynasty enjoyed Po Han Hu Xi (a mass water-sprinkling and song-and-dance activity in the ancient Western Regions) in the southern gate tower of Luoyang City. Polo that originates from Persia (the old name of Iran) was also introduced in the Heluo region. At that time, there was a court built at the foot of the northern hillside of the house of Wang Liwen who was a common person in Gaocheng County, Henan Province. "From summer to autumn, Emperor Xuan Zong of the Tang Dynasty played and watched ball games here" before he ascended to the throne. Later on, Emperor Zhuang Zong of the Tang Dynasty also played polo with princes and ministers in Luoyang court. Additionally, during the Tang Dynasty, just like during foreign polo, hitting the ball while riding a donkey was the normal practice in the Heluo region.

The exchange between the Heluo region and Southeast Asia has been associated with the gradual development of the Nanyue region. Southeast Asian countries frequently dispatched envoys to Luoyang to pay tribute during the Han and Wei dynasties. In September in the thirteenth year of Jianwu (37 AD) of the Eastern Han Dynasty, "the barbarians (in today's Cambodia) beyond the border of Ri'nan County have presented the imperial court with a white pheasant and a rabbit." It is the first emissaries from Southeast Asian countries recorded in *The Book of the Later Han*. Yavadvipa (present-day Java Island or Sumatra Island in Indonesia) and Dhara/Talaing (present-day Myanmar) also successively dispatched ambassadors to Luoyang. Meanwhile, according to various records, there were only four Southeast Asian countries that had contact with the Sui Dynasty. They included the Kingdom of LâmẤp (present-day Central Vietnam), Chitu (most scholars think that it's located in present-day Northern Malaysia), Chenla (present-day Cambodia), and Poli State (some think that it's located in present-day Kalimantan Island in Indonesia while others think that it's in present-

图6-5 伊川县出土四曲双鱼纹长杯

Figure 6-5　Silver and Gold Four-Lobed Dish with Two fishes, unearthed in Yichuan County, Luoyang

day Bali Island, Indonesia) respectively. After the Tang Dynasty, many poets in the Heluo region, such as Du Shenyan, Shen Quanqi, and Liu Yuxi, consecutively arrived in Annam (present-day Vietnam) and wrote numerous poems and articles.

Heluo culture has spread widely at home and abroad since its formation. Nationally, from the Yellow River basin to the Yangtze River basin, it has consistently migrated to the South and integrated with local cultures. Gradually, Hakka culture, Minnan culture, and Taiwan culture that have the same roots as Heluo culture have come into being, and Heluo culture has been extended to Southeast Asia through them. Additionally, Heluo culture has also been disseminated in the Korean Peninsula and Japanese Archipelago. Economic exchanges in the pre-Qin period and the Han dynasty, their imitation of the Heluo region's political systems in the Wei and Jin dynasties, and students dispatched to Luoyang in the Sui and Tang dynasties are all proof that Heluo culture exerted a far-reaching influence in these two countriess. Finally, Heluo culture spread from Luoyang, the eastern starting point of the Silk Road, to the Western Regions, Central Asia, Western Asia, and Europe. As the Imperial Capital of the Han, Wei, Sui, and Tang dynasties, Luoyang was at the center of cultural exchanges at the time.

During contemporary times, Heluo culture has become a calling card of cultural exchanges between china and the rest of the world. Since 1989, the International Conference on Heluo culture has been held fifteen times. These academic forums focus initially on Luoyang, then on Henan. Nowadays, they have expanded to include Guangdong, Taiwan, Jiangxi, Fujian, and other areas. Experts and scholars from both sides of the Taiwan Strait, Hong Kong, and Macao regions and the rest of the world, including Japan, South Korea, Singapore, Malaysia, America, Britain, Germany, Russia, Vietnam, Thailand, Australia, New Zealand, Philippines, Italy, Austria, Belgium, Brazil, and Argentina have actively participated in these conferences and enthusiastically exchanged views with each other. Moreover, some news media like *People's Daily* (the overseas edition), *Voice of Overseas Chinese*, and *Sing Tao Daily* of the United States have consecutively reported these spectacular conferences. Accordingly, Heluo culture has become the pioneer of Chinese culture "going global," a distinctive mark recognized by all Chinese people at home and abroad. Given that the Peony Culture Festival

图6-6　龙门东西山全景
Figure 6-6　Panoramic view of the West Hill in Longmen Grottoes

化"走出去"的先锋,成为海内外华人华侨民族认同的显著标识。随着中国洛阳牡丹文化节的持续举办,龙门石窟、隋唐大运河中心、丝绸之路东方起点等成为世界文化遗产,河洛文化为越来越多的中外游客所感知,所了解,所喜爱。"让洛阳走向世界,让世界了解洛阳"。河洛文化逐步走向全国、走向海外的交流互鉴过程,充分彰显其独特的人文价值和巨大的影响力。

of Luoyang, China, which has been held many times, Longmen Grottoes, the center of the Grand Canal of the Sui and Tang dynasties, the eastern starting point of the Silk Road, and so on, have become the World Cultural Heritage, Heluo culture has been known, understood and loved by an increasing number of Chinese and foreign tourists. They have not only made Luoyang go global but also let the world know Luoyang. Through mutual exchanges and learning, Heluo culture has gradually spread throughout the country and all over the world thereby showcasing its unique humanistic value and significant influence.

附录1：河洛文化大事记

约5300年前后

"河洛古国"遗址考古证明，河洛地区是当时最具代表性和影响力的文明中心。

公元前21世纪—前16世纪

禹之子启嗣位。启之子太康迁都斟鄩，仲康、夏桀也都斟鄩。二里头遗址出土有夏代青铜器以及酒器。河洛地区率先进入青铜器时代。

公元前16世纪—前11世纪

夏桀暴政，商汤灭夏，都西亳。偃师尸乡的西亳城是洛阳的第二座都城。

公元前11世纪

周武王元年，灭商，建周朝。周成王五年，召公、周公营建东都。周公在洛邑制礼作乐。

周平王元年（前770年）

平王废镐京，在秦襄公率师护送下来到洛邑。史称东周。

周敬王二年（前518年）

孔子与南宫敬叔入周，问礼于老子，访乐于苌弘。

汉高祖五年（前202年）

二月，刘邦于汜水称帝，定都洛阳。五月，刘邦改都长安。

王莽始建国四年（12年）

二月，王莽定洛阳为东都，长安为西都。

东汉建武元年（25年）

十月，刘秀至洛阳，以此为都城。史称东汉。

建武五年（29年）

始立太学于洛阳开阳门外，刘秀亲临太学观看。

Appendix 1: Heluo Cultural Events

About 5,300 years ago

The archaeological remains at the site of the Ancient Heluo Kingdom prove that the Heluo region was the most representative and influential civilization center at that time.

21st century BC - 16th century BC

Qi, Emperor Yu's son, succeeded the throne. Tai Kang, son of Emperor Qi, moved the capital to Zhenxun(present-day Luoyang), and Zhong Kang and Xia Jie also moved the capital to Zhenxun. Bronze and wine vessels made in the Xia Dynasty have been unearthed at Erlitou Site. That means the Heluo region took the lead in entering the Bronze Age.

16th century BC - 11th century BC

Xia Jie's tyranny led to the destruction of the Xia Dynasty by Shang Tang who was the founder of the capital in Xibo. Xibo in nowaday's Shixiang of Yanshi became another capital city in Luoyang.

11th century BC

In the first year of King Wu of Zhou, he destroyed the Shang Dynasty and built the Zhou Dynasty. In the fifth year of King Cheng of Zhou, the Duke of shao, and the Duke of Zhou built the eastern capital. The Duke of Zhou composed the system of rites and music in Luoyi.

The First Year of King Ping of Zhou (770 BC)

King Ping abolished the capital Haojing(present-day Xi'an) and was escorted by Duke Xiang of Qin to settle in Luoyang (called Luoyi then), starting the Eastern Zhou Dynasty.

The Second Year of King Jing of Zhou (518 BC)

Confucius and Nangong Jingshu came to the Zhou Dynasty and asked Lao Tzu about the rites. They also visited Chang Hong for music knowledge.

The Fifth Year of King Gao of Han (202 BC)

In February, Liu Bang became Emperor in Sishui and established the capital in Luoyang. In May, Liu Bang moved the capital to Chang'an.

王梁穿渠引谷水于洛阳城下。在王城东筑千金碣。

交趾太守锡光等相率遣使贡献于刘秀。

建武八年（32年）

高句丽王到洛阳。刘秀复其王位。

建武二十四年（48年）

穿阳渠，引洛水为漕，鸿沟水系通航。从此，洛阳南通江淮，东达齐鲁。

建武中元二年（57年）

倭奴国遣使奉献，刘秀赠"汉倭奴国王印"一枚，此为中日国家间正式往来之始。

永平八年（65年）

明帝遣郎中蔡愔等十八人，出使西域，拜佛求法。公元67年用白马驮经回到洛阳。永平十一年，明帝命筑白马寺。这是佛教传入我国之始。

永平十六年（73年）

明帝派遣班超等出使西域，镇抚西域各国。西域与汉断绝关系六十五年后，至此恢复，以洛阳为中心的"丝绸之路"开通。

建初九年（84年）

今柬埔寨境内的究不事国，派使臣到洛阳，赠送生犀等。

永元九年（97年）

掸国（今缅甸境内）王雍由调遣使来洛献贡，汉回赠金印、冠带。

永兴元年（105年）

宦官蔡伦，在洛阳制成"蔡侯纸"。

元初四年（117年）

张衡在洛阳制成浑天仪。

永和元年（136年）

扶余国王朝汉至京师。

The Fourth Year after Wang Mang Founded the State (12 AD)

In February, Wang Mang made Luoyang the eastern capital and Chang' an the western capital.

The First Year of Jianwu in the Eastern Han dynasty (25 AD)

In October, Liu Xiu went to Luoyang, settled there, and made it the capital, and founded the Eastern Han Dynasty.

The Fifth Year of Jianwu (29 AD)

The first Taixue(Imperial Academy) was set up outside Kaiyang Gate of Luoyang, which Liu Xiu had visited.

Wang Liang led the valley water through the canal to Luoyang City and made a *Jie* (stone tablet) worth a thousand gold in the East of King City.

Xi Guang, the administrator of Jiaozhi Commandery, and other ministers sent envoys to help Liu Xiu.

The Eighth Year of Jianwu (32 AD)

The king of Goguryeo went to Luoyang. Liu Xiu restored his throne.

The Twenty-fourth Year of Jianwu (48 AD)

By digging the Yang canal and borrowing water from the Luo River, the canal was open to navigation thereby connecting Luoyang with Jianghuai(the plain between the Yangtze and Huai Rivers) in the south and Qilu(present-day Shandong province) in the east.

The Second Year of Zhongyuan of the Jianwu Years (57 AD)

The Japanese emperor dispatched an ambassador to present slaves. Emperor Liu Xiu gave him a seal engraved with "King of the dependency of Japan". It is regarded as the beginning of official communication between China and Japan.

The Eighth Year of Yongping (65 AD)

Emperor Ming of the Han Dynasty dispatched Cai Yin to the Western Regions to pray to Buddha and request for the scriptures which were carried by the white horse in 67 AD. The emperor ordered to build the White Horse Temple in the eleventh year of Yongping's reign. The trip to the Western Regions represents the beginning of the introduction of Buddhism into our country.

The Sixteenth Year of Yongping (73AD)

Emperor Ming sent a group of people including Ban Chao to the Western Regions to guard and appease countries there, thereby restoring the relations that

延熹二年（159年）

天竺国（今印度境内）派使臣入洛阳。

延熹九年（166年）

大秦国王（古罗马帝国皇帝）安敦遣使臣入洛。此为中国与欧洲国家直接往来的开始。

熹平四年（175年）

灵帝诏蔡邕等正《六经》，刻石46块，立于太学，后人称之为"熹平石经"。

光和元年（178年）

二月，汉灵帝诏置洛阳鸿都门学。开创我国文艺学艺术院校的先河。

魏黄初元年（220年）

魏王曹丕废献帝，自立为帝，国号魏，都洛阳。

正始二年（241年）

魏齐王于太学立古文、小篆、隶书"三体石经"，刻石28块，又称"正始石经"。

正元元年（254年）

马钧在洛阳发明龙骨水车。

景元三年（262年）

司马昭在洛阳杀竹林玄学的代表人物嵇康。

晋泰始元年（265年）

司马炎取代曹魏，自立为帝，国号晋，史称西晋。

泰始四年（268年）

扶南（今柬埔寨）、林邑（今越南南方）各派使臣入洛阳，向晋入贡。

北魏太和十七年（493年）

孝文帝率军进驻洛阳，第二年定都洛阳。

had been severed for 65 years. The Silk Road, with Luoyang as its starting point, was established from then on.

The Ninth year of Jianchu (84 AD)

The emperor of the country of Jiu Bu Shi (present-day Cambodia) dispatched ambassadors to Luoyang and sent rhinoceroses to the Han Dynasty.

The Ninth Year of Yongyuan (97 AD)

King Yong You of Dan country (present-day Burma) dispatched ambassadors to Luoyang to pay tribute and the emperor of the Han Dynasty sent a golden seal, a hat, and a belt in return.

The First Year of Yongxing (105 AD)

Cai Lun, the eunuch of the Han Dynasty, invented Cai Hou Paper in Luoyang.

The Fourth Year of Yuanchu (117 AD)

Zhang Heng invented the armillary sphere in Luoyang.

The First Year of Yonghe (136 AD)

The King of Fu Yu country visited the capital of the Han Dynasty.

The Second Year of Yanxi (159 AD)

Tianzhu (present-day India) sent envoys to Luoyang.

The Ninth Year of Yanxi (166 AD)

An Dun, the king of Da Qin (an ancient Roman emperor), sent envoys to Luoyang. This was the beginning of direct contact between China and European countries.

The Fourth Year of Xiping (175 AD)

Emperor Ling gathered ministers like Cai Yong to revise the *Six Classics* which were engraved on 46 stones in Taixue. Later generations call them "Stone Classics of the Xiping Reign."

The First Year of Guanghe (178 AD)

Emperor Ling of the Han Dynasty issued an edict to set up Hongdumen School in Luoyang in February, which became the trailblazer in the establishment of literature and art schools.

The First Year of Huangchu of Wei State in the Three-Kingdom Period (220 AD)

King Cao Pi of Wei state deposed Emperor Xian of the Eastern Han

附录图1-1 函谷关 刘龙/摄

Appendix Figure 1-1　The Hangu Pass Archaeological Site Museum　Photo by Liu Long

Dynasty, usurped the throne, and changed the national title to Wei, and made Luoyang the capital.

The Second Year of Zhengshi (241 AD)

Emperor Qi(namely Cao Fang)of the Kingdom of Wei ordered the inscription of "Three-script Stone Scripture" with classical pre-Qin script, the small seal script, and the clerical script in the 28 stone tablets, otherwise known as "Zhengshi Stone Scripture."

The First Year of Zhengyuan (254 AD)

Ma Jun, a famous Chinese inventor of the Three Kingdom Period, invented the dragon-bone water liftin Luoyang.

The Third Year of Jingyuan (262 AD)

Sima Zhao, a powerful minister in the Kingdom of Wei, killed Ji Kang (one of the representatives of the Bamboo Grove Metaphysics) in Luoyang.

The First Year of Taishi of the Jin Dynasty(265 AD)

Sima Yan dethroned the King of the Wei Kingdom and made himself the King, declaring the beginning of the Western Jin Dynasty with the title of "Jin."

The Fourth Year of Taishi (268 AD)

Funan (present-day Cambodia) and Linyi (present-day south of Vietnam) sent ambassadors to Luoyang and paid tribute to the Jin Dynasty.

The Seventeenth Year of Taihe of the Northern Wei Dynasty (493 AD)

Emperor Xiaowen led his army and stationed them at Luoyang, and made Luoyang the capital.

The Ninth Year of Taipingzhenjun (448 AD)

Kou Zhiqian, the celestial master of Taoism, passed away this year. He lived in seclusion at Songshan Mountain for as long as thirty years.

The First Year of Jingming (500 AD)

Binyang Cave was dug and statues were built at Longmen West Hill.

The First Year of Xiping (516 AD)

Queen Hu ordered to build Yongning Temple in November.

The Fifth Year of Wuding (547 AD)

The book *Record of Buddhist Temples in Luoyang* was completed by Yang Xuanzhi.

太平真君九年（448年）

道教天师寇谦之仙逝。寇谦之潜心隐居嵩山修道，历时三十年。

景明元年（500年）

洛阳龙门西山开凿宾阳中洞石窟并造像。

熙平元年（516年）

冬十一月，胡太后诏制永宁寺。

武定五年（547年）

杨衒之《洛阳伽蓝记》成书。

隋仁寿四年（604年）

十一月，隋炀帝杨广来洛阳视察地形，遂定洛阳为东京。

大业元年（605年）

三月，命杨素、宇文恺营建东京洛阳，五月建西苑。发河南诸郡男女百余万，开通济渠，此为隋唐大运河开凿之始。

大业二年（606年）

十月，建洛口仓。十二月，置回洛仓。是年，炀帝下诏将全国善乐舞者，集于洛阳。是年，炀帝设进士科，为中国科举之始。

大业三年（607年）

三月，派遣朱宽出使琉球。八月，日本国遣小野妹子至洛阳。

大业四年（608年）

三月，百济、赤土（马六甲）遣使奉献。隋遣常骏出使赤土。四月，遣裴世清出使日本。是年，日本药师惠日等人来洛学医。

大业五年（609年）

正月，改东京为东都。

唐显庆二年（657年）

正月，高宗李治来洛阳，以洛为东都。

上元元年（674年）

于阗王伏阇雄、波斯王卑路斯入朝至洛阳。

The Fourth Year of Renshou of the Sui Dynasty (604 AD)

In November, Emperor Yang of the Sui Dynasty, Yang Guang, inspected the terrain in Luoyang and decided that Luoyang would be the eastern capital.

The First Year of Daye (605 AD)

Yang Su and Yuwen Kai were designated to build the eastern capital, Luoyang, in March. In May, they completed the construction of Xiyuan, the imperial garden. Besides, they gathered millions of Henan County people to dig the Tongji Canal which is often regarded as the start of the construction of China's Grand Canal of the Sui-Tang dynasties.

The Second Year of Daye (606 AD)

Luo Kou Granary was built in October, while Huiluo granary was built in December. Emperor Yang issued an edict to gather good dancers and musicians all around the country in Luoyang. Besides, he set up Jin Shi examination, which was the beginning of the Imperial Civil Examination System.

The Third Year of Daye (607 AD)

A Chinese ambassador, Zhu Kuan, was dispatched to Liu Qiu (present-day Taiwan) in March. OnonoImoko, a Japanese ambassador, arrived in Luoyang in August.

The Fourth Year of Daye (608 AD)

In March, Paekche and Chitu (present-day Malacca) dispatched envoys to pay tribute to the imperial court. Meanwhile, Chang Jung was dispatched to Chitu by the Sui Dynasty. This was followed in April by the dispatch of Pei Shiqing to Japan. In the same year, Meguhi, a senior pharmacist, and other Japanese people came to Luoyang to study medicine.

The Fifth Year of Daye (609 AD)

In the lunar January, "Dongjing" was changed to "Dongdu" (Both mean the eastern capital in Chinese).

The Second Year of Xianqing of the Tang Dynasty (657 AD)

In the first month of the lunar year, Li Zhi (Emperor Gao Zong) came to Luoyang and named it the Eastern Capital.

The First Year of Shangyuan (674 AD)

Yuchi Fuduxiong, the king of Khotan, and Pirooz, the emperor of Persia, became officials of the imperial court and arrived in Luoyang.

上元二年（675年）

十二月，龙门卢舍那大佛立，武则天助脂粉钱两万贯。

垂拱四年（688年）

十二月，明堂建成，号曰万象神宫。

武周天授元年（690年）

二月，武则天在洛城殿对贡士进行考试，自此开始了历代贡士参加殿试的制度。

九月，武则天降睿宗为皇嗣，自立为帝，国号周，洛阳为"神都"。

天册万岁元年（695年）

四月，天枢铸成，号曰："大周万国颂德天枢"。

长安元年（701年）

拂菻遣使臣来洛。

长安二年（702年）

日本遣使入洛阳献贡。

开元二十一年（733年）

玄宗李隆基在洛阳接见了日本第八次遣唐使。

开元二十三年（735年）

日本第九次遣唐使到达洛阳，受到唐玄宗的接见。

天宝三年（744年）

李白与杜甫在洛阳相会。

乾元二年（759年）

杜甫因往来于洛阳、华州之间，目睹兵荒马乱，民不聊生之景，于是写出《三吏》，《三别》等名篇。

大和二年（828年）

白居易寓居洛阳履道坊，结九老诗社，修龙门伊水八节滩等。在洛阳居住十八年。

The Second Year of Shangyuan (675 AD)

In December, the statue of Vairocana Buddha was completed in Longmen Grottoes. Empress Wu Zetian donated 20,000 strings of coins, money for her cosmetics, to sponsor the building of the statue.

The Fourth Year of Chuigong (688 AD)

The Ming Palace was built in December and was initially named the Celestial Palace

The First Year of Tianshou of the Wu-Zhou Dynasty (690 AD)

Empress Wu Zetian personally assessed Second-Degree Scholars in the Hall of Luo Cheng in February. The inaugural session was the initiation of the system of final imperial examination presided over by the emperor.

In September, Wu Zetian demoted Emperor Rui Zong from emperor to crown prince and assumed the title of "Empress." The title of her reigning dynasty was Zhou and Luoyang was named "the Divine Capital."

The First Year of Tiance Wansui (695 AD)

In April, Tianshu was built and engraved with "Tianshu, the monument in praise of virtue around the country."

The First Year of Chang'an (701 AD)

Byzantine Empire sent emissaries to Luoyang.

The Second Year of Chang'an (702 AD)

Japan dispatched envoys to Luoyang to present a tribute to the imperial court.

The Twenty-first Year of Kaiyuan (733 AD)

Li Longji, Emperor Xuan zong had the eighth interview with Japanese ambassadors in Luoyang.

In the twenty-third year of Kaiyuan (735AD)

Emperor Xuan Zong granted an interview to Japanese envoys in Luoyang for the ninth time.

The Third Year of Tianbao (744 AD)

Li Bai and Du Fu met in Luoyang.

The Second Year of Qianyuan (759 AD)

Du Fu traveled between Luoyang and Huazhou and witnessed the turmoil and chaos of war and the masses living in misery. So he wrote "Three Officers", "Three Partings" and other well-known works.

后梁开平三年（909年）

正月，朱温以洛阳为京都。

后唐同光元年（923年）

十二月，后唐迁都洛阳。

后晋天福二年（937年）

石敬瑭打败后唐，将都城迁到洛阳。

北宋雍熙元年（984年）

日本奈良东大寺僧人来华，于洛阳晋谒宋太宗，并赠书。

至道二年（996年）

赐嵩阳书院敕额和监本《九经》。

熙宁五年（1072年）

日本僧人成寻率弟子七人乘船人宋，在西京洛阳延和殿被神宗见。

熙宁六年（1073年）

程颢、程颐讲学于洛阳，全国各地求学者络绎不绝。

熙宁十年（1077年）

理学家邵雍卒于洛阳，谥康节。

元丰七年（1084年）

十二月，司马光在洛完成《资治通鉴》。

北宋之后

洛阳远离王朝中心，河洛文化进入衰落期。

The Second Year of Dahe (828 AD)

Bai Juyi, who made his home in Lvdaofang, organized the Nine Elder Poetry Club and constructed the Bajietan on the Yi River in Longmen Mountain. He lived in Luoyang for as long as eighteen years.

The Third Year of Kaiping of the Later Liang Dynasty (909 AD)

In January of the lunar calendar, Zhu Wen founded the later Liang Dynasty, with Luoyang as its capital.

The First Year of Tongguang of the Later Tang Dynasty (923 AD)

In December, the later Tang Dynasty moved its capital to Luoyang.

The Second Year of Tianfu of the Later Jin Dynasty (937 AD)

Shi Jingtang overthrew the later Tang Dynasty and established the later Jin Dynasty and made Luoyang its capital.

The First Year of Yongxi of the Northern Song Dynasty (984 AD)

Buddhists of Todai-ji of Nara, Japan, came to China. They were received by Emperor Tai Zong of the Song Dynasty in Luoyang, and presented books to the emperor.

The Second Year of Zhidao (996 AD)

Emperor Tai Zong of the Song Dynasty gave Songyang Academy horizontal inscribed boards and nine Confucian classics of the official version.

The Fifth Year of Xining (1072 AD)

Jojin, a famous Japanese monk, led seven followers sailed China in the Song Dynasty. They were summoned by Emperor Shen Zong at the Yanhe Palace, Luoyang, the western capital at that time.

The Sixth Year of Xining (1073 AD)

Cheng Yi and Cheng Hao gave lectures in Luoyang. Scholars from all over the country flooded there to study from them.

The Tenth Year of Xining (1077 AD)

Shao Yong, a renowned Confucian philosopher and who's posthumous title is Kangjie, died in Luoyang.

The Seventh Year of Yuanfeng (1084 AD)

In December, Sima Guang finished his great work *Comprehensive Mirror for Aid in Government*.

After the Northern Song Dynasty

Luoyang was no longer the center of nation. Heluo Culture started to decline..

附录2：中国历史年代简表

Appendix2: A Brief Chronology of Chinese History

中国历史年代简表

A Brief Chronology of Chinese History

五帝时代 Period of the Five Legendary Rulers c. 2600 BC-c. 2070 BC	黄帝 Huangdi (Yellow Emperor)	
	颛顼 Zhuanxu	
	帝喾 Diku (Emperor Ku)	
	尧 Yao	
	舜 Shun	
夏 Xia Dynasty	c. 2070 BC-c. 1600 BC	
商 Shang Dynasty	c. 1600 BC-c. 1046 BC	
西周 Western Zhou Dynasty	c. 1046 BC-c. 771 BC	
东周 Eastern Zhou Dynasty 770 BC-256 BC	春秋 Spring and Autumn Period	770 BC-476 BC
	战国 Warring States Period	475 BC-221 BC
秦 Qin Dynasty	221 BC-206 BC	
汉 Han Dynasty 206 BC-220 AD	西汉 Western Han	206 BC-25 AD
	东汉 Eastern Han	25 AD-220 AD
三国 Three Kingdoms 220 AD-280 AD	魏 Wei	220 AD-265 AD
	蜀汉 Shu Han	221 AD-263 AD
	吴 Wu	222 AD-280 AD
晋 Jin Dynasty 265 AD-420 AD	西晋 Western Jin	265 AD-317 AD
	东晋 Eastern Jin	317 AD-420 AD

续表 Continued Table

南北朝 Southern and Northern Dynasties 420 AD-589 AD	南朝 Southern Dynasties	宋 Song	420 AD-479 AD
		齐 Qi	479 AD-502 AD
		梁 Liang	502 AD-557 AD
		陈 Chen	557 AD-589 AD
	北朝 Northern Dynasties	北魏 Northern Wei	386 AD-534 AD
		东魏 Eastern Wei	534 AD-550 AD
		北齐 Northern Qi	550 AD-577 AD
		西魏 Western Wei	535 AD-556 AD
		北周 Northern Zhou	557 AD-581 AD
隋 Sui Dynasty		581 AD-618 AD	
唐 Tang Dynasty		618 AD-907 AD	
五代十国 Five Dynasties and Ten States	五代 Five Dynasties 907 AD-960 AD	后梁 Later Liang	907 AD-923 AD
		后唐 Later Tang	923 AD-936 AD
		后晋 Later Jin	936 AD-947 AD
		后汉 Later Han	947 AD-950 AD
		后周 Later Zhou	951 AD-960 AD
	十国 Ten States 902 AD-979 AD	北汉 Northern Han	951 AD-979 AD
		吴 Wu	902 AD-937 AD
		吴越 Wuyue	907 AD-978 AD
		闽 Min	909 AD-945 AD
		南汉 Southern Han	917 AD-971 AD
		荆南（又称"南平"）Jingnan (Nanping)	924 AD-963 AD
		楚 Chu	927 AD-951 AD
		南唐 Southern Tang	937 AD-975 AD
		前蜀 Former Shu	907 AD-925 AD
		后蜀 Later Shu	934 AD-965 AD

续表 Continued Table

宋 Song Dynasty 960 AD-1279 AD	北宋 Northern Song	960 AD-1127 AD
	南宋 Southern Song	1127 AD-1279 AD
辽 Liao (契丹 Qidan/Khitan)	907 AD-1125 AD	
西夏 Xixia (Tangut)	1038 AD-1227 AD	
金 Jin	1115 AD-1234 AD	
元 Yuan Dynasty	1206 AD-1368 AD	
明 Ming Dynasty	1368 AD-1644 AD	
清 Qing Dynasty	1616 AD-1911 AD	
中华民国 Republic of China	1912 AD-1949 AD	
中华人民共和国 People's Republic of China	1949 AD-	